Curriculum Focus

Ourselves

Terry Jennings

HOPSCOTCH EDUCATIONAL PUBLISHING

Curriculum Focus series

History

Toys Key Stage 1
Famous Events Key Stage 1
Famous People Key Stage 1
Invaders Key Stage 2
Tudors Key Stage 2

Geography

Islands and Seasides Key Stage 1
The Local Area Key Stage 1

Science

Ourselves Key Stage 1
Plants and Animals Key Stage 1
Materials Key Stage 1

Published by Hopscotch Educational Publishing Ltd,
Unit 2, The Old Brushworks, 56 Pickwick Road,
Corsham, Wilts SN13 9BX
Tel: 01249 701701

© 2004 Hopscotch Educational Publishing

Written by Terry Jennings
Linked ICT activities by Michelle Singleton
Series design by Blade Communications
Illustrated by David Burroughs
Cover illustration by Claire Boyce
Printed by Colorman (Ireland) Ltd

Terry Jennings hereby asserts his moral right to be identified as the author of this work in accordance with the Copyright, Designs and Patents Act, 1988.

ISBN 1-904307-56-6

All rights reserved. This book is sold subject to the condition that it shall not, by way of trade or otherwise, be lent, hired out or otherwise circulated without the publisher's prior consent in any form of binding or cover other than that in which it is published and without a similar condition, including this condition, being imposed upon the subsequent purchaser.

No part of this publication may be reproduced, stored in a retrieval system, or transmitted, in any form or by any means, electronic, mechanical, photocopying, recording or otherwise, without the prior permission of the publisher, except where photocopying for educational purposes within the school or other educational establishment that has purchased this book is expressly permitted in the text.

Contents

	Cross-curricular links	4
	Introduction	5
1	Our bodies	6
2	Our senses	13
3	Growing and changing	34
4	Differences	42
5	Movement	50
6	Living and non-living	59
7	Food and drink	67
8	Exercise	75
9	Medicines and drugs	83

Cross-curricular links

Chapter	Science	Citizenship	Literacy framework	Numeracy framework	ICT SoW
1	Unit 1A		Y1, Term 1: W8		Unit 1C Unit 2A
2	Unit 1A		Y1, Term 1: W8 Y1, Term 2: W5, W10 Y1, Term3: W8		Unit 2B
3	Unit 1A		Y1, Term 2: W10		Unit 1C
4	Unit 1A		Y1, Term 1: W8 Y1, Term 2: W5		Unit 2A
5	Unit 1A		Y1, Term 1: W8 Y1, Term 2: W5		Unit 1C
6	Unit 1A	Unit 5	Y1, Term 1: W8	Solving problems – organising and using data	Unit 2C
7	Unit 1A		Y1, Term 1: W8 Y1, Term 2: W5		Unit 1A
8	Unit 2A		Y1, Term 1: T15 Y1, Term 2: T25		Unit 1D
9	Unit 2A		Y1, Term 2: T25 Y1, Term 3, T19, T20	Solving problems – organising and using data	Unit 1E
10	Unit 2A		Y1, Term 1: W8 Y1, Term 2: W5 Y1, Term 2: T25		Unit 1C
11	Unit 2A		Y1, Term 1: W8 Y1, Term 2: W5		Unit 1D
12	Unit 2A	Unit 4	Y1, Term 1: W8 Y1, Term 2: W5 Y1, Term 2: T25		Unit 1D

Introduction

Curriculum Focus: Ouselves helps to make science fun by giving you (especially those of you who are not science specialists) the support you need to plan stimulating and exciting lessons.

This book will help you to plan and teach a unit of work based on the QCA Scheme of Work for Science at Key Stage 1. Also, where appropriate, this book gives indications as to how the work can be linked with other areas of the curriculum.

The material in this book gives you a sound foundation from which to plan a unit of work for your classes.

The material includes:

- detailed **Teachers' notes** giving **background information** on each topic and/or concept to be taught;
- fully illustrated **Generic sheets** offering a wealth of resource material that can be used again and again;
- **Lesson plans** full of ideas for introducing and developing the lesson;
- photocopiable and **differentiated Activity sheets** to support individual and group work.

We recognise that there will be different levels of attainment among the children and that their developing literacy skills will require different levels of support during individual and group work. To help you provide activities that meet the needs of your classes, each chapter contains three photocopiable sheets based on the same material, but for children of different levels of attainment. This enables the whole class to take part in a similar activity.

- Activity sheet 1 in each chapter is intended for lower-attaining children.
- Activity sheet 2 is suitable for most children.
- Activity sheet 3 challenges the higher-attaining children.

Young children have a natural curiosity about themselves and their bodies – their height, weight, hair, eye colour, birthdays and likes and dislikes fascinate them. As a result, they bring a good deal of their own knowledge and understanding to a study of the body. These ideas need to be carefully explored in order to prevent misunderstandings, while at the same time they present ideal opportunities to develop the children's knowledge and experience.

The activities in this book offer opportunities to examine some of the body parts and to discuss their function and, later, to see how some of these parts help us to survive. The activities also provide the background information that will enable the children to explore the similarities and differences between humans and to look at growth and the human life cycle. They also explore ways in which we can stay healthy by eating a varied diet and avoiding substances that could be harmful to the body.

During the course of this work the children will gain experience in questioning, observing, comparing, predicting, recording, measuring and drawing conclusions. They will also have opportunities to work cooperatively and to share their ideas with others.

It almost goes without saying that great care and sensitivity is needed in any work where children compare themselves, and their bodies or their lifestyles, with those of other people. It is also important for the sake of their future happiness and wellbeing, particularly when discussing bodily parts and such functions as excretion, defaecation and reproduction, that children do not come to associate any part of their bodies with adult disapproval.

There are some ideas for taking children's photos. check your school policy and whether you should obtain permission from parents or carers first.

CHAPTER 1

Our bodies

TEACHERS' NOTES

Humans and other mammals

Humans belong to a group of animals called mammals. Mammals are warm-blooded, which means they maintain a steady body temperature, whatever the external temperature may be.

The main characteristic of mammals is mammary glands in the skin of the females. These secrete milk for the young. Mammals are backboned animals (vertebrates) and in most species the young are not hatched from eggs but born alive from within the mother. Many mammals have an insulating layer of hair which prevents excessive loss of heat, but humans, whales, porpoises, dolphins and seals are much less hairy. Some mammal species have spines or scales instead of hair.

Humans have a jointed internal skeleton made up of bones, with muscles attached to them to enable movement. (See Chapter 5 for more information on the skeleton, muscles and movement.) We are totally bipedal – in other words, the body is fully and continuously balanced on the two hind limbs. We have two arms, hands and fingers. One small but significant difference between humans and our closest relatives, the apes and monkeys, is our long thumb. All the apes and monkeys have so-called opposable thumbs – thumbs that can bend across the palm – but the human thumb is especially long. This makes it possible for us to carry out delicate tasks. Another advantage we have over our ape and monkey relatives is our large brain. We are probably the most intelligent animal species that has ever lived.

Various parts of our body are used for the senses: ears for hearing, nose for smelling, eyes for seeing, tongue for tasting and skin for feeling. (See Chapter 2 for more information on the senses.)

Cells, tissues, organs and systems

Like all living things, a human body is made up of building blocks called cells. Most cells are so small that they can only be seen through a powerful microscope. There are more than 50 billion cells in a human body. The largest is the human egg, which is about the size of a printed full stop.

An organ is a collection of tissues with a particular job to do. For instance, the heart pumps blood and the stomach and liver help to digest food.

More than one organ is needed to digest food. The stomach does some of the work, but the mouth, intestines, liver, pancreas and other organs also help. These various organs form the digestive system. The heart, veins and arteries are organs of the blood system or circulatory system. They work together to circulate blood around the body. A number of different systems go to make up the human body. They include the skeletal, muscular, digestive, nervous, excretory, respiratory, circulatory, reproductive and endocrine systems.

In addition

Other features of mammals include:

- an external part to the ear, known as the pinna;
- different types of teeth to chew, grind or chop food;
- toes or fingers that terminate in nails, claws or hoofs;
- a well-developed brain;
- a muscular sheet, called the diaphragm, which separates the chest from the abdomen and is used in breathing.

Most mammals also have sweat glands in the skin, and as the sweat evaporates it takes away heat, helping to cool the animal's body.

Unlike all other animals, we humans have a complicated language with which we communicate our ideas to others. We are able to store information in written records and, more recently, by other means, and to pass it on from one generation to another. We can work out the answers to questions and difficult problems and also make and use tools and machines.

Humans have a long postnatal development. After a gestation period of nine months, one baby (but occasionally larger numbers of offspring) is born which suckles for periods of up to several years before weaning, depending upon cultural practices. The rate of development is slow and the period of childhood prolonged, which has a great influence on the family and social organisation of the human race.

Technical terms

Humans have bodies with similar parts. Key Stage 1 children need to be familiar with the following words:

Body, head, hair, forehead, cheek, chin, ear, eye, nose, mouth, neck, shoulder, arm, elbow, wrist, hand, finger, thumb, leg, knee, ankle, foot, heel, toe, waist.

1 GENERIC SHEET

Our bodies

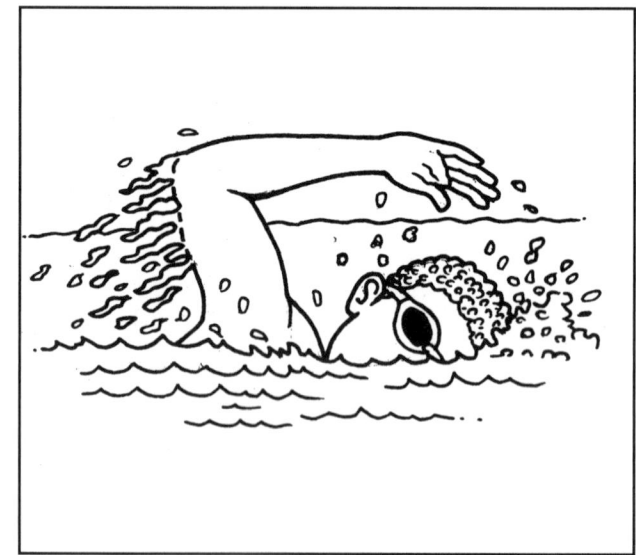

8 CURRICULUM FOCUS • OURSELVES

PHOTOCOPIABLE

Our bodies

LESSON PLAN

> **Science objective (Unit 1A)**
> • To know that humans have bodies with similar parts.

Resources

- A large cut-out picture of a person, or a shop dummy
- Tie-on labels
- Coloured pencils or crayons
- Generic sheet 1 (page 8)
- Photocopiable activity sheets 1–3 (pages 10–12)

Starting points: *whole class*

Gather the children around the cut-out figure or dummy. Point to a part of the model's body and ask them to point to the same part on their own bodies. Invite them to name that part and, if successful, to tie a label on the appropriate part of the model. Parts could include head, arms, legs, hand, foot, fingers, toes and face.

Introduce the game 'Simon says'. This provides a quick and easy means of assessing the children's level of knowledge. You could put the more able children at the back of the class to prevent the less knowledgeable children from copying them.

Show the children Generic sheet 1 which has pictures of people carrying out different activities. Ask them to say which part or parts of the body are being used for each activity.

Group activities

Activity sheet 1
This sheet is for children who need more support. They are required to study the outline of the human body and to label the parts using the words provided.

Activity sheet 2
This sheet is aimed at children who can recognise more external features than in Activity sheet 1.

Activity sheet 3
This sheet allows the children free rein to use their knowledge of bodily parts. They are also required to demonstrate, in writing, some knowledge of the functions of parts of the body.

Plenary session

Ask a volunteer to lie on a large sheet of paper and draw around him or her. Cut out the entire life-size shape and then carefully cut off the limbs and head from the body shape and label all the parts. Challenge the children to reassemble the body, like a puzzle. If desired, this activity can be treated as a race to put the body back together again, using a timer. Discuss what we use the different parts of the body for.

Ideas for support

Produce a display of photographs and other pictures showing people with the parts of their bodies labelled. The parts of a large doll could be similarly labelled.

Ideas for extension

Make a collection of dolls and similar articulated figures. Make a 'dolls' hospital', using shoe boxes as beds. Let the children decide which part of the body on each figure is ill or injured. Label the 'bed' accordingly and perhaps put a small paper bandage on the injured part.

Plan more opportunities for activities that involve naming parts of the body, such as 'Raise your hands', 'Lift one leg', 'Touch your neck' and 'Shake your foot'. These can be incorporated into a classroom lesson or linked with a PE activity.

Name _____

Know your body

Name the parts of the body.
Join the words to the correct parts.

elbow

foot

head

arm

leg

hand

knee

neck

Now point to all these parts on your own body.

10 CURRICULUM FOCUS • OURSELVES

ACTIVITY SHEET 1

PHOTOCOPIABLE

Name _____

Know your body

2 ACTIVITY SHEET

Name the parts of the body. Use the word bank to help you.
Write the names in the correct places.

Word bank
head   knee   foot   neck   hand   leg   elbow   wrist
arm   chin   waist   shoulder   forehead   mouth   hair

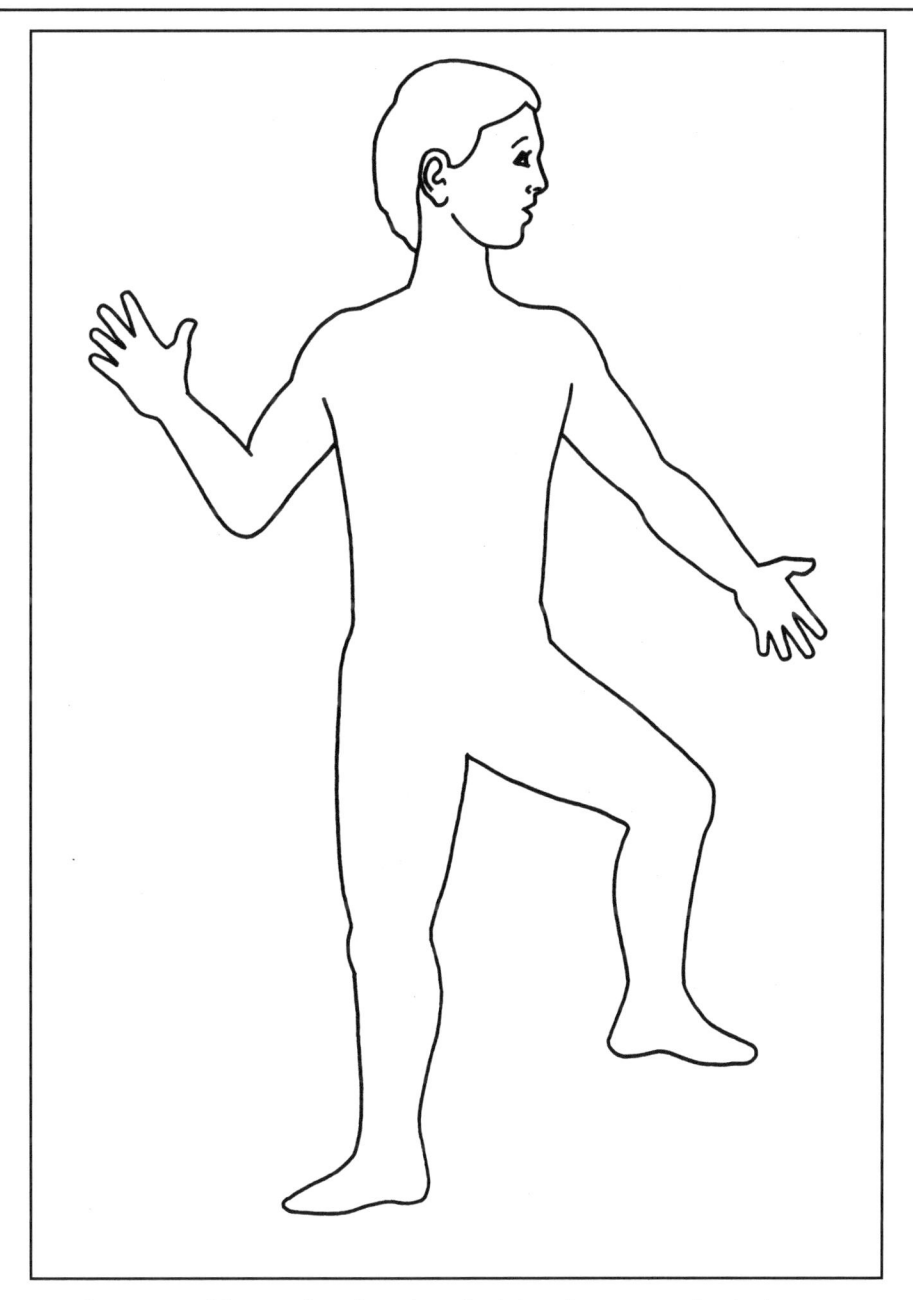

Draw a picture of yourself on the back of this sheet. Label the parts.

PHOTOCOPIABLE

CURRICULUM FOCUS • OURSELVES   11

Name _____

Know your body

3 ACTIVITY SHEET

Name as many parts of the body as possible. Label them.

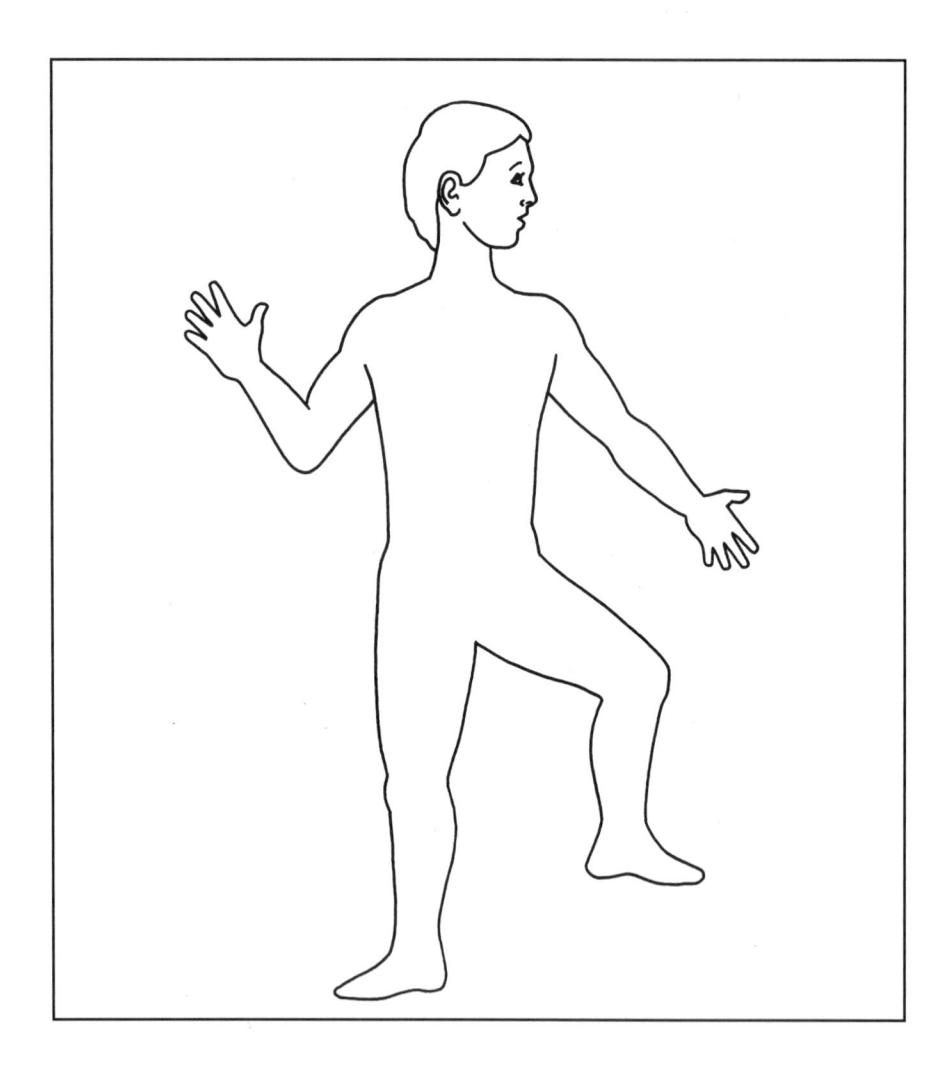

Choose four parts of the body. For each part, say what we use it for.

1 _____
_____

2 _____
_____

3 _____
_____

4 _____
_____

12   CURRICULUM FOCUS • OURSELVES   PHOTOCOPIABLE

Our senses

CHAPTER 2

TEACHERS' NOTES

Senses and sense organs

Even the simplest living thing must adjust to its surroundings and avoid danger, find food and recognise its own kind. It is the function of our senses to make us aware of changes in our surroundings and also of changes within our own bodies.

All over our bodies we have sense cells that respond to stimuli. A stimulus is a change in light, pressure, temperature, chemical concentration or some other factor, which produces a reaction in an animal (or plant). Structures that respond to the stimuli are called receptors, and they pass on nervous impulses, or 'messages', to which the body responds. Some of these receptors are scattered throughout the skin, while others are concentrated in special sense organs such as the eyes and ears. It is often said that we have five senses: sight, hearing, smell, taste and touch. However, we also have a sense of balance, located within our ears. The sense of touch is really a combination of four sensations: contact, pressure, temperature and pain. The receptor cells to touch are present all over the skin, although their number varies from place to place. There are, for instance, far more touch cells on the lips and fingertips than on the backs of the hands.

Although the sense organs are vital parts of our bodies and those of other animals, not all the receptors are equally important. The eyes and ears are obviously of great importance to people, as is the sense of touch; taste and smell are of lesser importance, although whole industries are founded on the pleasures these senses can bring – the confectionery, brewing, perfume and cosmetics industries among them. If we lose one of our senses, our other senses may be intensified to compensate for it. People who have lost their sight, for example, develop enhanced senses of hearing and touch. Deaf people develop keen senses of touch and sight and can often 'hear' music by means of the vibrations it produces in solid objects.

It is important to remember that our senses not only bring us pleasure, but they also protect us. We can see and hear danger; we can smell poisonous gases or taste many substances that are harmful. We can taste and smell if food and drinks are bad or 'off'. Even pain, that most unpleasant of sensations, warns us that something is wrong and signals us to take steps to protect our bodies. Unfortunately, once the damage is done the pain often continues.

Eyes and eyesight

In humans and other primates, the eyes are set at the front of the head, with each eye giving a slightly different view of the same object. These views are turned into stereoscopic or three-dimensional images, to enable us to judge distances accurately. Stereoscopic vision is most highly advanced in hunting and tree-dwelling animals. In herbivores, such as deer, antelope, sheep and rabbits, the eyes are on the sides of the head, to give a much wider but less detailed field of view.

A human eyeball is about 2.5cm in diameter and it weighs only about 7g. The pupil at the centre of the eye is a hole that allows light to enter the interior of the eye. The iris, the coloured part of the eye, changes the size of the pupil, which in turn controls how much light enters the eye. In dim light the pupils open wide; in bright light the pupils close so that only a tiny opening is left.

The lens in the eye focuses an inverted image of the object on the retina at the back of the eye. On the retina there are special receptors which receive light and transmit information to the brain. There are two types of receptors, known as rods and cones. The rods are affected by light intensity and are used mainly for night vision. They can only detect shades of grey. The cones are used in daylight and are sensitive to colours. Humans, along with apes and monkeys, are among the minority of mammals that are able to see colours. The nerve cells in the retina pass messages to the brain and the inverted image on the retina is interpreted the right way up by the brain.

Our eyes are well protected against injury. Each eye is encased in a bony socket padded with fat, while tears, eyelids and eyelashes wash off and brush off dirt. Muscles attached to the tough outer coat, or sclera, of the eye at one end and the eye socket at the other, swing the eyeball around in its socket. They also keep the eye moving slightly all the time. The brain ignores messages from the eye unless they are constantly changing. In this respect the eye is more like a Closed Circuit Television (CCTV) camera than a stills camera.

Ears and hearing

Sounds travel as vibrations, and our ears collect vibrations in the air and change them into nerve signals that are passed to the brain. The outer ear, the part of the ear we can see, leads into an ear canal that ends in a very thin membrane called the eardrum. The human outer ear is flat and generally not movable, unlike that of some other animals. Nevertheless, it helps to direct the sound vibrations down to the eardrum. When the sound vibrations hit the eardrum they make it move. The movement of the eardrum is passed on to three tiny bones which transmit the vibrations to another membrane called the oval window. In doing so, the ear bones amplify the sound vibrations. These vibrations are passed from the oval window into a coiled tube known as the cochlea. This is filled with fluid and lined with tiny hair-like sense cells. As these sense cells move, they send electrical signals to the brain where the signals are analysed and interpreted by the brain as sound.

Our ears are very good at working out the direction of a sound. They do this by noticing the difference in the timing of the arrival of a sound at each ear. We can detect differences as small as one ten-thousandth of a second and use this information to help locate a sound. We cannot detect all sounds, however. Many animals, including dogs, mice, bats and dolphins, can hear sounds that are too high pitched for us to hear.

The ear also has the important function of controlling our sense of balance. Above, and attached to, the cochlea are three semicircular canals. These are fluid-filled tubes set at right angles to each other. Whenever you move your head, the fluid moves in at least one of these canals, and it is this movement of fluid that stimulates tiny nerve endings in the semicircular canals. These in turn send nervous impulses to the brain, thus ensuring that we stay upright and balanced. If, however, you spin round fast, the fluid in the semicircular canals continues moving, even though you may have stopped. Your brain thinks you are still moving and everything around you seems as if it is still spinning, so that you feel dizzy.

In addition to hairs, the ear canal is lined with wax that helps to protect the eardrum. Nevertheless, objects pushed into the ears can easily damage the eardrum, as can loud noises.

Smelling and tasting

The senses of smell and taste are both involved with the detection of chemicals. Chemicals in the air are picked up by receptors in the nose. Chemicals in food are detected mostly in the mouth.

High up inside the nose is the olfactory organ, which is responsible for the sense of smell. It consists of two small areas of cells which have tiny hair-like detectors, called cilia, attached to them. The cilia wave around in a film of mucus. All molecules of the chemical substance being smelled have to dissolve in the mucus before they can be detected by the sensory cells of the olfactory organ. A message is then sent to the brain. Sniffing is necessary for the air to reach the olfactory organ.

Although it is often said that our sense of smell is poor compared with that of cats, dogs and many other mammals, it is still believed that we are able to smell the difference between more than 10,000 different odours. The sense of smell is readily fatigued, however, so that after a few minutes' exposure to a new smell it is no longer perceived, although newcomers will detect it at once.

The sense of taste is located in the taste buds on the tongue, on the roof of the mouth, the insides of the cheeks and at the back of the mouth. Only chemicals soluble in water can affect the taste buds, by dissolving in the moisture in the mouth. The solutions enter pores in the taste buds and stimulate sensory cells that send messages to the brain. Although all taste buds appear to be identical in structure, each one is sensitive to only one of the four tastes – sweet, sour, salt and bitter. These are not evenly distributed over the tongue, so that some parts of the tongue are more sensitive to a particular chemical than others.

The wide variety of flavours attributed to food result from the simultaneous stimulation of the taste buds of the tongue and the olfactory organs of the nasal cavity. When we have a blocked nose, because of a cold, our food has little or no taste.

As well as taste, the tongue is also sensitive to touch, heat, cold and pain, and much of our information about food depends on its texture and temperature as well as its taste. Hot food is more easily tasted than cold and, in addition, has more flavour.

Touching and feeling

The skin is a complicated organ covering the surface of the body. It is made up of many parts and has many functions, one of which is to act as a sense organ. The sense of touch really includes all the sensations we feel with our skin – touch, pressure, heat, cold and pain.

Often you feel one or more of these basic sensations. When you open the door to the freezer, you feel the cold. When you take an ice cube out of the freezer, you not only feel the sensation of cold but also that of touch.

The top layers of the skin are called the epidermis. Just below this are the sensory cells that detect temperature. One set of cells detects coldness and another set detects warmth. Both types are found all over the body. There are more temperature sensory cells in the fingers and lips than in other places. This means that the fingers and lips are best for sensing temperature. As with all of the basic kinds of sensation, the response comes from electrical impulses to the brain, triggered when the receptor cell is stimulated.

Also near the surface of the skin are touch sensory cells. Some of them are joined to hair follicles, the so-called 'roots' of hairs. The touch cells can detect the touch of a feather. Again, there are a great number of these sensory cells in the skin of the fingers. We use these cells to feel the surface of objects.

The lower layers of the skin are called the dermis. Deep down in the dermis are pressure sensory cells. These respond to a heavier 'touch' than the touch cells. When something pushes against the skin, the pressure cells will send electrical impulses to the brain.

Some sensory cells in the skin and inner parts of the body may also work when they sense a very strong stimulus. They may send impulses to the 'pain centre' of the brain. If a very strong stimulus starts thousands of the ordinary sensory cells working at once, this may cause you to feel pain. Pain is 'useful' because it lets us know when something is wrong with a part of the body or prevents us damaging ourselves.

Which sense?

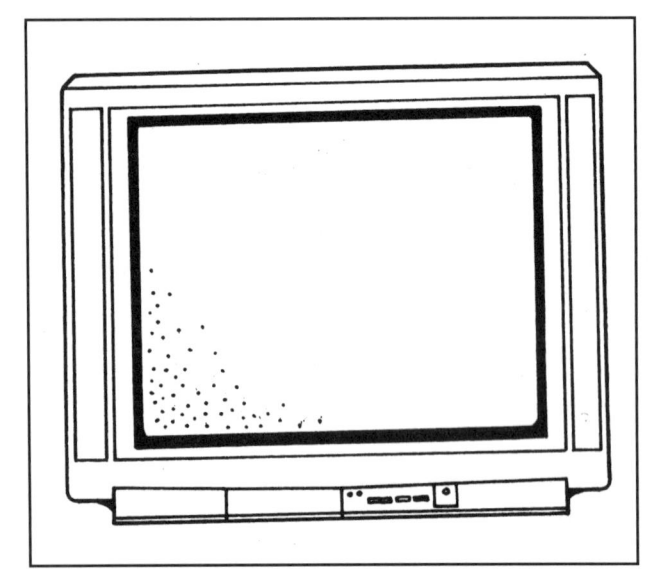

Noise

Which do you like?

3 GENERIC SHEET

Put a tick next to the sounds you like and a cross next to the sounds you do not like.

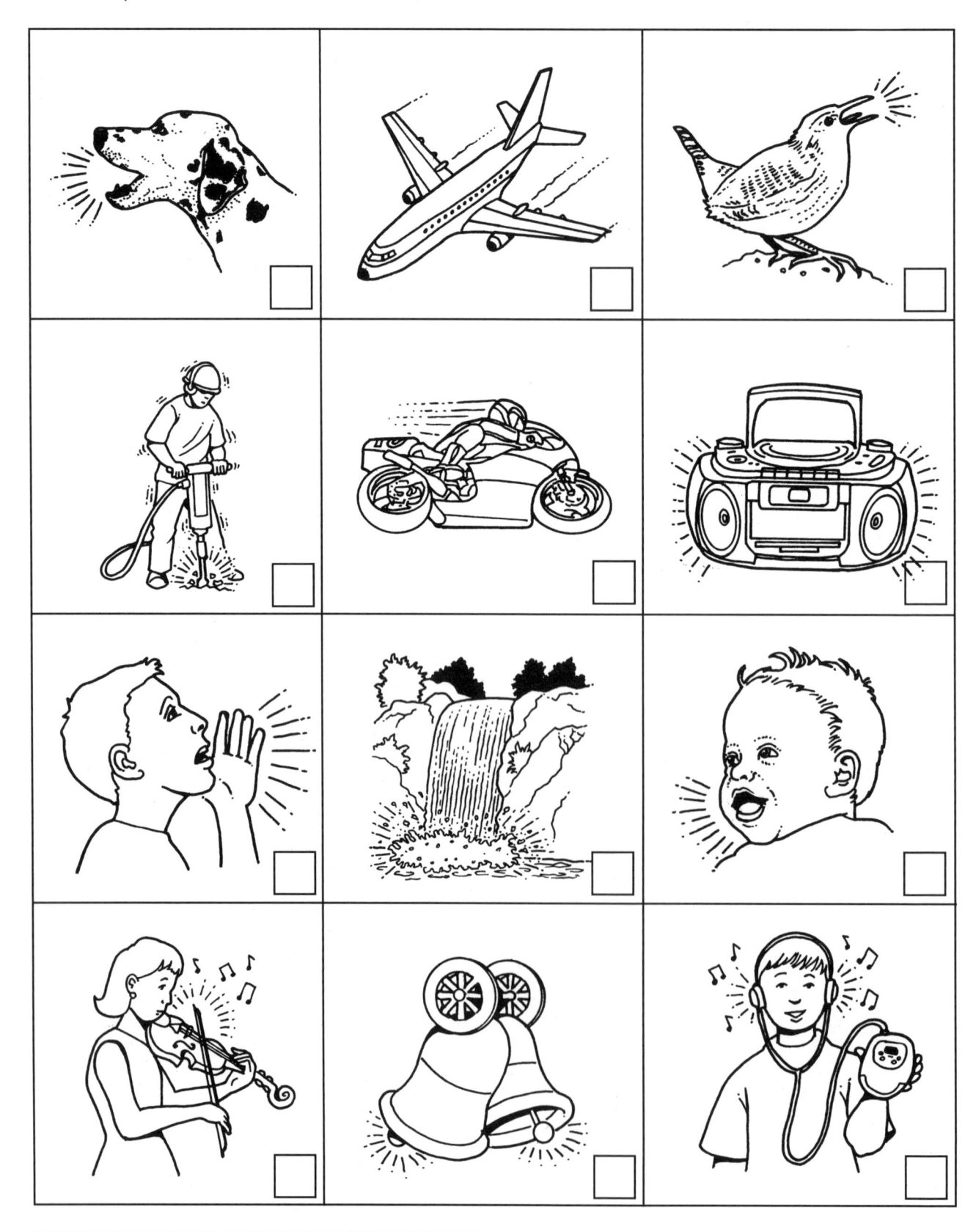

Our senses

LESSON PLAN 1

Science objective (Unit 1A)
• To learn that we have five senses which allow us to find out about the world.

Resources
- A large picture of a garden or a food shop
- Generic sheets 1–3 (pages 16–18)
- Activity sheets 1–3 (pages 21–23)

Starting points: *whole class*

Hold up an object, such as a hoop or ball from PE. Ask the children to describe what you are holding. Ask them how they are able to describe it. Agree that it is because they can see it. Explain that to do this we have to use our senses; in this case we are using the sense of sight.

Go on to discuss the different senses and how they help us. Say that we call these senses 'seeing', 'hearing', 'smelling', 'tasting' and 'touching'. List these on the board. Display a large copy of Generic sheet 1 and together discuss which of our senses we need to use each object illustrated. Guide the children towards an awareness that for some of the objects, such as the television and the flower, we use more than one sense; we see and hear the television and we see and touch and smell the flower.

Invite some volunteers to the front of the class. Give them some objects to describe from behind a screen so that the rest of the class cannot see them. Ask the volunteers to take it in turns to choose an object and describe it by its appearance, smell, texture, the sound it makes, and so on. The other children have to identify the object.

Ask the children to think about the sense of hearing. Is everything we hear a nice sound? Show them the picture on Generic sheet 2 and discuss the sounds that are depicted there. How many of them are unpleasant sounds? Likewise, are all smells pleasant? Is everything we see beautiful?

Tell the children they are now going to do an activity on recognising which part of their body is used for which sense.

Group activities

Activity sheet 1
This sheet is aimed at children who can recognise the link between pictures of the five main sense organs and some of the sensations they are used to detect.

Activity sheet 2
This sheet is aimed at children who can recognise the link between the names of the five main senses and some of the sensations they are used to detect.

Activity sheet 3
This sheet is for the more able children. They have to recognise the five main senses and some of the sensations they are used to detect. They are also asked to write down some more occasions when they use these five senses.

Plenary session

Discuss how our senses tell us what is happening around us. Talk about some of the ways in which our senses give us pleasure, such as when eating a favourite food, smelling a flower or stroking a pet animal. Discuss how our senses warn us of danger – for example, sirens, bells, traffic lights, pedestrian crossings, the smell of burning or of bad food, and so on.

Ideas for support

Make a classroom display of objects that can be identified using each of the five main senses. Have a feely box and change the object inside regularly.

Create a labelled frieze of the local area, showing the different sights (nice and nasty), sounds (pleasant and unpleasant) and smells (pleasant and unpleasant).

Ideas for extension

Ask the children to write down how the five senses would help them to enjoy a lovely meal.

Use the senses to sort and classify a variety of materials.

In pairs, let one of the children be blindfolded. Each blindfolded child should describe to his or her partner what it feels like, then swap places. With careful supervision, the blindfolded child of each pair could try to walk around the classroom or playground, with the second child acting as guide. Then let the blindfolded child try to identify some small, safe objects. Let them try to identify different sounds, such as someone's voice or a tap running.

Be sensitive to the needs of visually impaired children. Some children who do not seem to know their colours could be colour blind. Remind the children that it is dangerous to look directly at the sun or other bright lights.

Linked ICT activities

Add one object at a time to the feely bag and ask the children to put their hand into the bag and describe what they can feel. Using a program with a word bank, such as 'Clicker', 'Talking Write Away' or 'Textease', create a word bank with words that the children might use to describe what they can feel in the bag – hard, rough, smooth and so on.

Using a digital camera, ask the children to take a photograph of the object in the bag after they have tried to guess what was in it. Then, using the word bank, ask them to create some sentences that describe the object they can feel in the bag.

Create a wall display with the title 'Guess what's in the bag'. Print out the children's descriptions under the heading 'What am I?'. Print out the photographs of the objects in the bag and stick them on the wall. See if the children can match the descriptions of the object to the correct picture.

Our senses

ACTIVITY SHEET 1

Draw a line from each object to the sense or senses you would use for it.

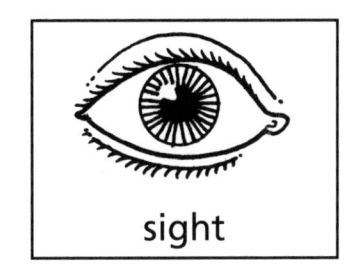

sight

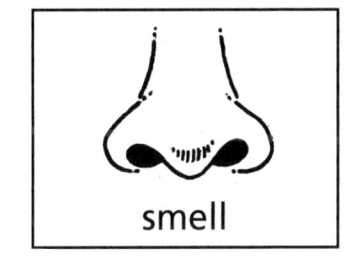

smell

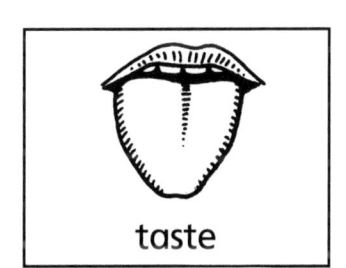

taste

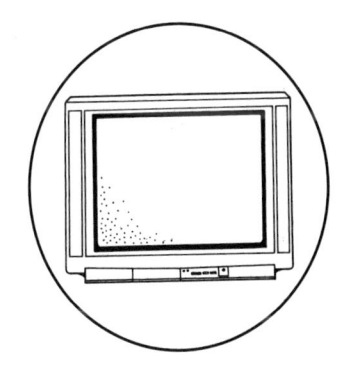

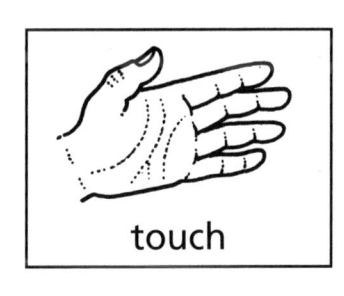

touch

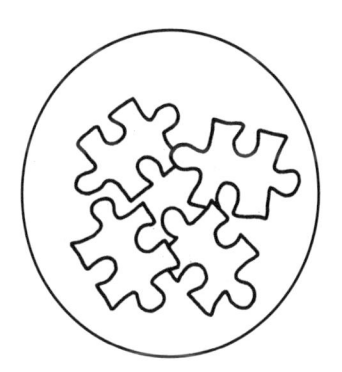

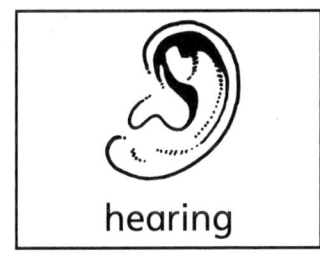

hearing

PHOTOCOPIABLE

CURRICULUM FOCUS • OURSELVES 21

Name

Our senses

2 ACTIVITY SHEET

Draw a line from each object to the sense or senses you would use for it. In the empty circles draw different things that are used by the senses. Link them to the correct senses.

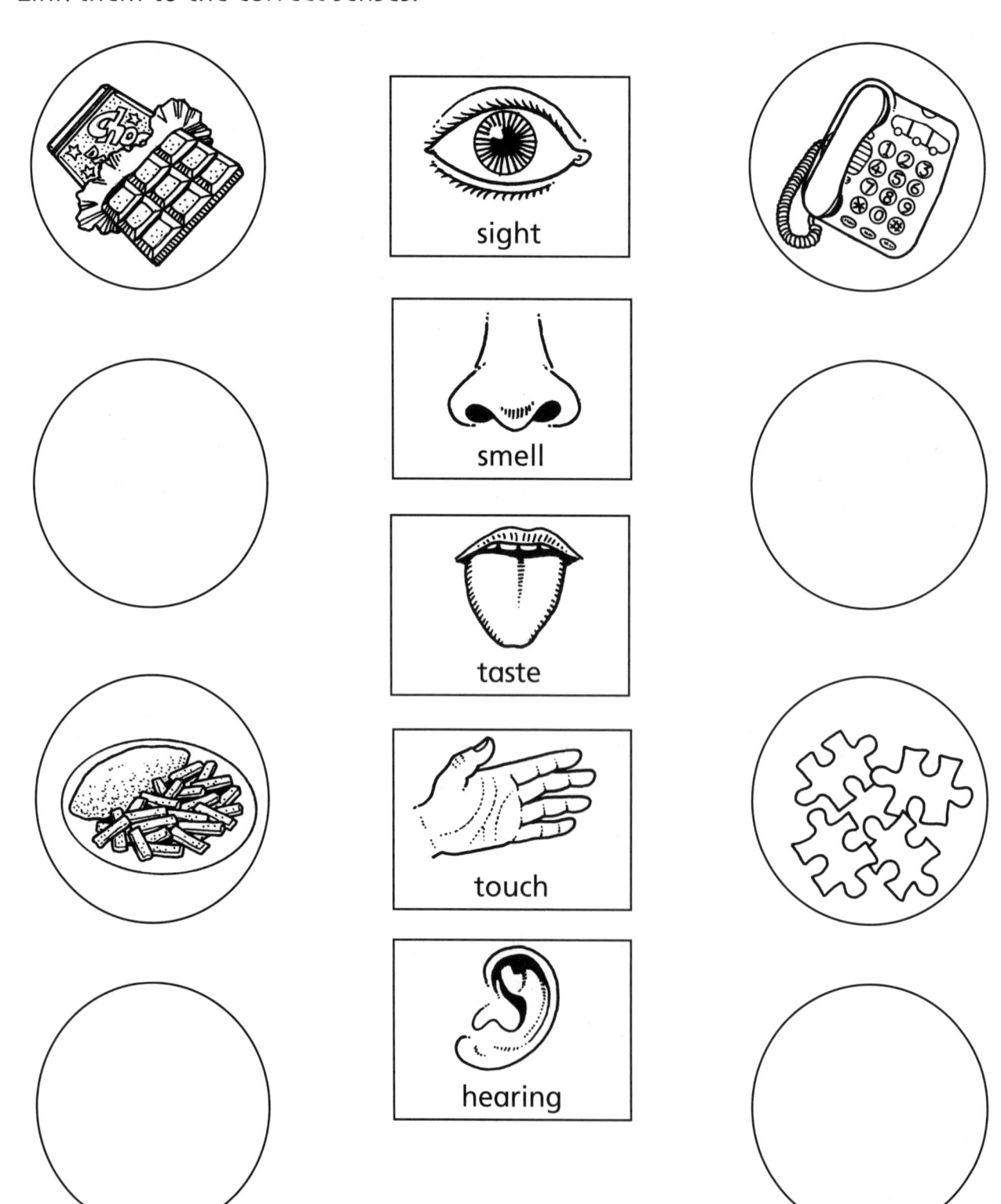

sight

smell

taste

touch

hearing

22 CURRICULUM FOCUS • OURSELVES

PHOTOCOPIABLE

Name _____

Our senses

3 ACTIVITY SHEET

Draw a line from each object to the sense or senses you would use for it.

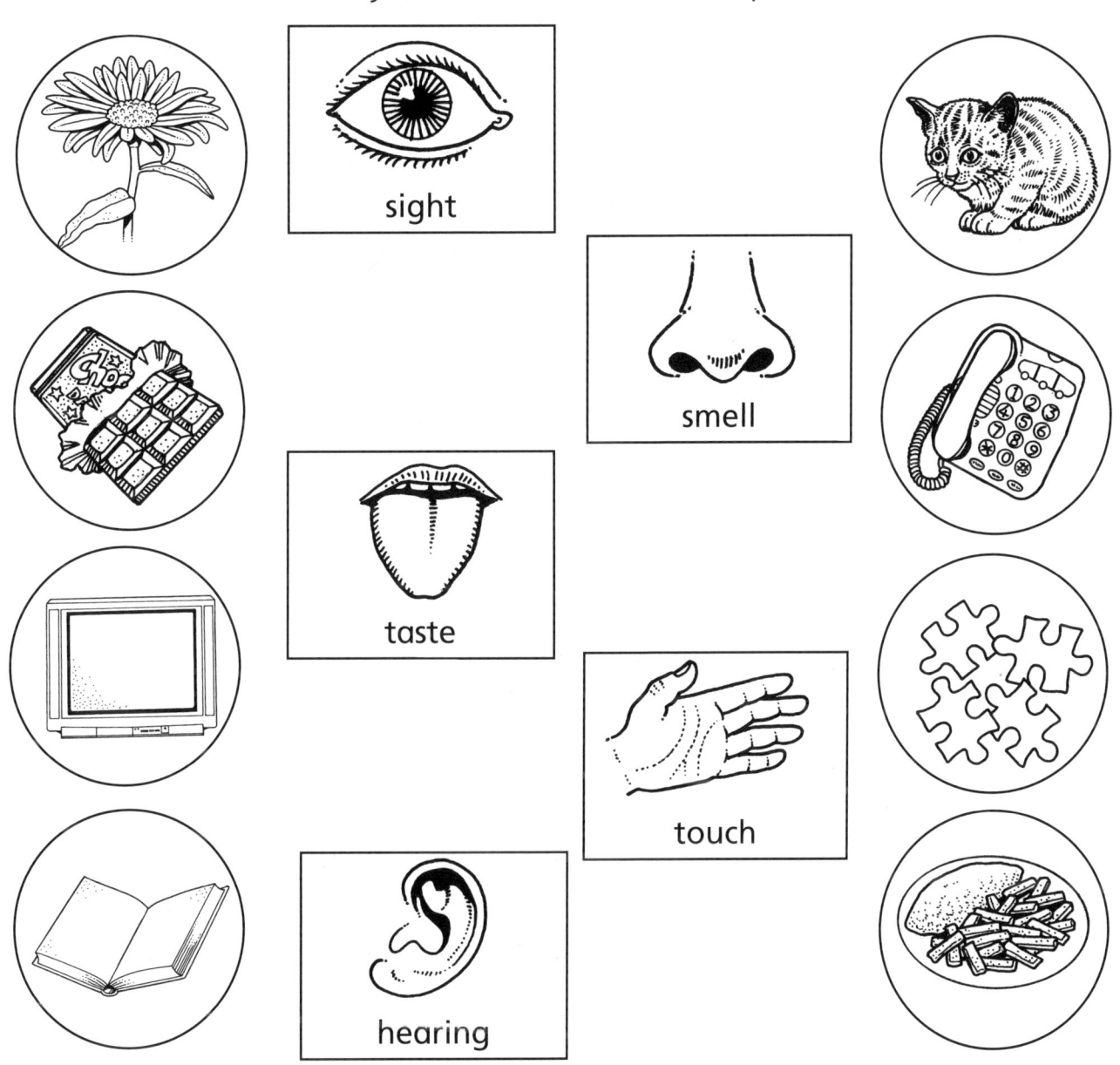

sight

smell

taste

touch

hearing

Which sense did you use most?

Write down some more times when you use your senses.

Seeing _____

Hearing _____

Touching _____

Smelling _____

Tasting _____

PHOTOCOPIABLE

2 LESSON PLAN

We need light to see

> **Science objective (Unit 1D)**
> • To understand that light is essential for seeing things.

Resources

- Shoe boxes with lids (as many as possible) painted black inside. Cut a 'window' 2cm across in one end
- Cardboard tubes (as many as possible) with one end covered by black paper held in place with an elastic band
- Torches
- Small objects, such as LEGO bricks, small figures, marbles, pens and pencil sharpeners
- Sunglasses and safety spectacles or goggles
- Activity sheets 1–3 (pages 26–28)

Starting points: *whole class*

Before the lesson, put small, easily identifiable objects, such as a pair of glasses and a pair of scissors, in the shoe boxes and cardboard tubes and place them around the classroom.

Ask the children how we are able to see things. From their existing knowledge of the senses they should know that we use our eyes. Talk about how we have to look after our eyes. Remind them that they should never look directly at the sun or other bright lights. Say that when the sun is very bright sunglasses can make us feel more comfortable. Demonstrate the action of sunglasses. People who drill or weld metals, scientists and other people who do work where something could get in their eyes, wear goggles for protection, as also do motorcyclists. Show the children the safety spectacles or goggles.

Discuss how some people cannot see. This may have been from birth or happened after birth. These people are said to be blind.

Ask the children to examine the cardboard tubes and shoe boxes in turn, without touching them, and try to say what is in each. Now provide them with a small torch. Again, let them try to identify the objects in each container.

Ask them to explain why they could see the objects in the containers with the torches, but could not see them without these sources of light. Establish that we can only see when there is light.

If possible go outside the school and talk about what the children can see. If you can't go outside, ask the children to tell you what they have seen outside the school and draw these on the board. Point out the road, lamp-posts (not lit up), cars (without their lights on), lollipop person, people passing by, houses and so on. Ask the children to tell you what would be different about this scene at night. (Lights on in houses, on cars, in lamp-posts; not so many people walking by; no lollipop person and so on.)

Tell the children they are going to do an activity about the difference between our world during the day and at night.

Group activities

Activity sheet 1
This sheet is aimed at children who can recognise the differences between night and day in the picture. They simply have to put a cross against the things which are different in the night time picture.

Activity sheet 2
This sheet asks the children to complete the drawing showing what the daytime scene would look like at night.

Activity sheet 3
This sheet is for the more able children. They have to complete the night time scene and also to list all the sources of light shown in both pictures.

Plenary session

Ask the children what they understand by 'darkness'. They should be able to recognise that darkness is the absence of light. Discuss the implications of not having light for road safety. If possible, close the curtains and switch off the lights in the classroom. Can the children still see things clearly? Switch on the lights again, one at a time. Can the children still see things clearly with increasing numbers of lights? Talk about the various natural and artificial sources of light, including the sun, stars, torches and other electric lights, candles, fires, and so on.

Ideas for support

Make a display of pictures showing scenes in the daytime and at night.

Ideas for extension

Repeat the group activity by placing different coloured objects in the darkened shoe boxes or cardboard tubes to see which colour shows up best.

Examine artificial sources of light and test the effectiveness of different types of reflective clothing in torchlight in a darkened room.

Linked ICT activities

Using a graphics program, such as 'Dazzle', tell the the children that they are going to create a daytime picture of a sunny day. Talk to them about what they might see outside the house: the road, the trees, garden and so on. Talk to them about what colours they might expect to use to paint a sunny day picture. Ask them to choose a colour for the background of the picture. Show them how to use the fill tool to fill the background of the picture and to change the colour of the background to show a sunny day and a dull day and to change the colour of the background to show a daytime picture and a night time picture. Show them some night time pictures so they can see how the changes in colour might change the picture.

Use a digital camera to record pictures that show the same scene in the daytime and at night. Let the children choose to paint a daytime or a night time picture. Show them how to use the drawing tools to create the foreground to the picture.

Name _____

What is the difference?

ACTIVITY SHEET 1

Here is a school in the daytime.

Here is the same school at night.

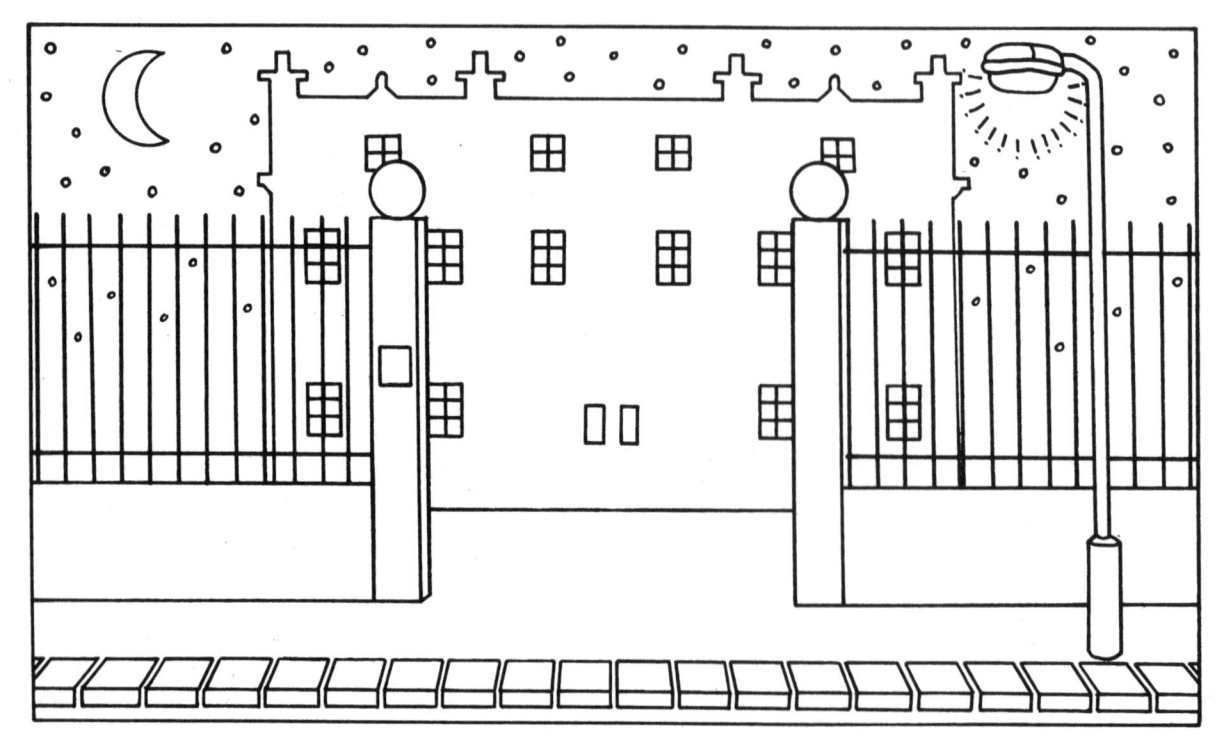

Put a cross against the things in the second picture that are different.

Name _____

What is the difference?

ACTIVITY SHEET 2

Here is a school in the daytime.

Now draw the school at night.
Colour your picture.

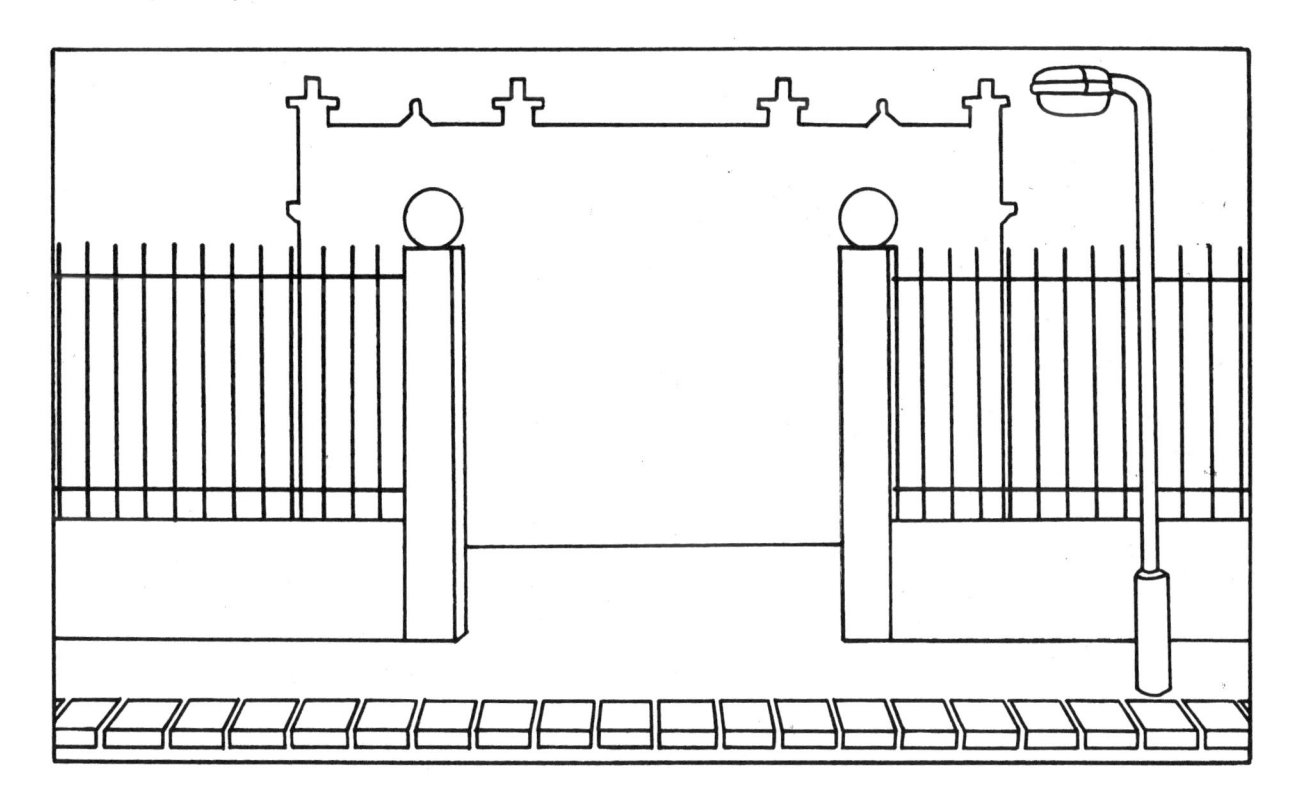

PHOTOCOPIABLE

CURRICULUM FOCUS • OURSELVES   27

Name _____

What is the difference?

ACTIVITY SHEET 3

Here is a school in the daytime.

Now draw the school at night. Colour your picture.

List the things in the two pictures that are giving out light.

a) _____

b) _____

c) _____

28   CURRICULUM FOCUS • OURSELVES   PHOTOCOPIABLE

Ears and hearing

LESSON PLAN 3

Science objectives (Unit 1F)
- To explore sounds using their sense of hearing.
- To understand that we hear with our ears.

Resources
- A tape recording of everyday sounds
- A musical instrument, such as a xylophone or Indian bells
- Hats, scarves, hoods or earmuffs
- Pictures of animals with large ears
- Stiff paper
- Adhesive tape
- Scissors
- Generic sheet 3 (page 18)
- Activity sheets 1–3 (pages 31-33)

Starting points: *whole class*

Talk to the children about their sense of hearing. Play the tape recording of everyday sounds. After each sound, stop the recorder and ask them to name the object that produced the sound.

Play a musical instrument, such as a xylophone or Indian bells. Ask the children what they think will happen if they put their hands over their ears. Ask them to do this, covering first one ear and then both. Repeat this activity using scarves, hats, ear muffs or hoods to cover the ears.

Now ask them to close their eyes and listen very carefully. They mustn't peep. Tiptoe to various parts of the room and make small sounds. Ask them to point to where the sound is coming from. Agree that our ears can also tell us which direction sounds are coming from.

Ask questions such as 'Was that a loud sound?', 'Was that a nice sound?' and 'Was that a soft sound?'

Discuss whether the children think we would hear better if we had larger external ears. Look at some pictures of animals with large ears. Discuss why it is important for these animals to hear well.

Help the children to make ear trumpets from stiff paper. Let them work in pairs to investigate whether the ear trumpet helps them to hear better. What happens when they turn the ear trumpet towards a soft sound?

Encourage the children to investigate the effect of cupping their hands in front of, and then behind their ears. Can they hear soft sounds better?

Following on from the work in Lesson 1, remind the children about the fact that there are sounds we like and sounds we don't like. Organise them into pairs and ask them to complete Generic sheet 3.

Now tell them they are going to do an activity that helps them to identify different types of sound.

Group activities

Activity sheet 1
This sheet asks the children to classify sounds into 'loud', 'soft', 'nice' and 'nasty'.

Activity sheet 2
This sheet is similar to the first, but the children are then asked to arrange four sounds in order of loudness.

Activity sheet 3
This sheet is for the more able children. They are required to arrange more sounds in order of loudness and to think of other sounds made by their mouths.

Plenary session

Discuss with the children what they have learned. Ask them to draw or write about the things that prevent us from hearing properly or help us and other animals to hear better. Discuss how our sense of hearing warns us of danger. Emphasise the fragility of the eardrum and the dangers of putting things into the ears.

Ideas for support

If there are children in the class with hearing impairments, they may need an extra helper or classroom assistant to sit with them and help them to identify the sounds.

Make a display of pictures of animals with large external ears.

Ideas for extension

Let the children watch television for a few minutes without the sound. Does this give them some insight into what it is like to be deaf?

Talk about deaf children and how a hearing aid sometimes helps them. Discuss the use of microphones and loudspeakers to amplify sounds.

Take the children on a 'listening walk'. Ask them to describe or write down what they can hear at each stopping place.

Linked ICT activities

Show the children how to use a tape recorder to record sound. Tell them that the computer can also record sounds. Using the sound recorder in Microsoft Windows, plug a microphone into the computer and show the children how to record their own voices. Show them other computer programs and CD-Roms which may contain sounds.

Using a program such as 'Textease' or 'Clicker 4', show the children how they can use the sounds from the sound bank to add to their words and pictures on the writing areas. Add some pictures to the blank page on the computer screen and ask the children to find the correct sound from the sound bank to match the pictures. Show them how to drag and drop the sound onto the page. Ask them to create their own picture page for their friend to find the sounds to match the pictures.

Name _____

Ears and hearing

1 ACTIVITY SHEET

Look at these pictures. Use the words in the box to write underneath each one what sort of sound it is. You might use more than one word.

| loud   soft   nice   nasty |

What is your favourite sound? _____

_____

PHOTOCOPIABLE

CURRICULUM FOCUS • OURSELVES   31

Name _____

Ears and hearing

2 ACTIVITY SHEET

Look at these pictures. Write underneath each one what sort of sound it is. You might use more than one word.

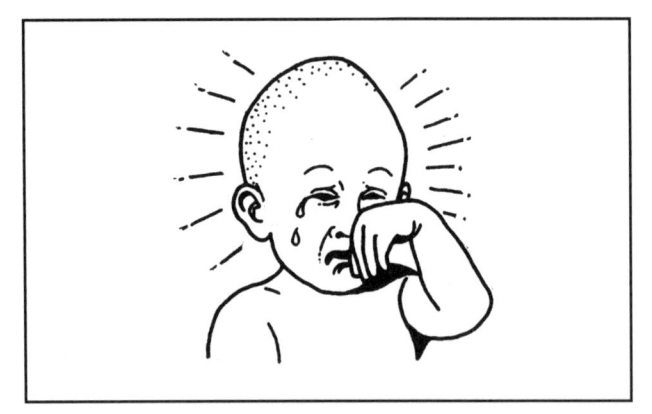

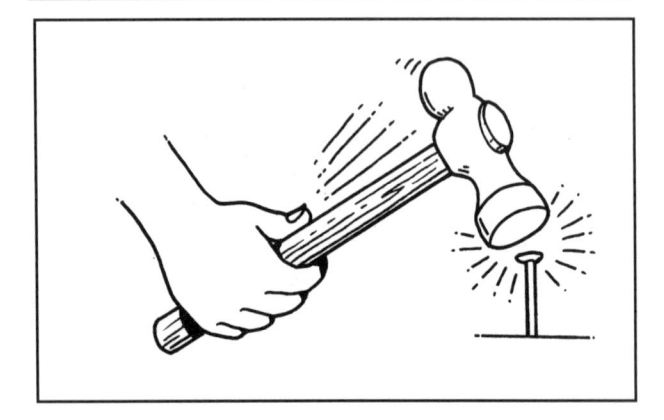

What is your favourite sound? _____

Put these sounds in order, from the softest to the loudest.

        say   shout   whisper   scream

_____

32 CURRICULUM FOCUS • OURSELVES   PHOTOCOPIABLE

Name _____

Ears and hearing

ACTIVITY SHEET 3

Draw something in each box that makes a sound. Give each one a caption to describe the sound. One has been started for you.

What is your favourite sound? _____

Put these sounds in order, from the softest to the loudest.

    bellow   say   shout   whisper   call   scream

_____

Think of some more sounds we make with our mouths. List them on the back of this sheet.

PHOTOCOPIABLE

CURRICULUM FOCUS • OURSELVES   33

Chapter 3: Growing and changing

TEACHERS' NOTES

Humans are animals

It is important that children understand that the animal kingdom includes fish, reptiles, mammals, birds, insects and amphibians and that humans are mammals and therefore animals.

Human reproduction

Instead of squirting a large number of eggs into water, as do fish and amphibians, or laying relatively large eggs with a chalky covering, human females produce minute eggs (each about the size of one of the full stops on this page) which are fertilised inside the mother's body and retained there until the young have grown large enough to be born.

The life of every human being then follows a common pattern from birth to death – infancy, childhood, the teenage years or adolescence, maturity and, finally, old age. We all experience the gradual transition from each of these stages to the next, unless our life is foreshortened by accident, illness or violence.

Throughout our lives our bodies and behaviour change. The most rapid changes take place during infancy, childhood and adolescence – from the moment of birth until the time we reach adult height and weight at the end of our teenage years. Then, for 40 or more years, as mature adults, our bodies change more slowly. Finally, as we enter old age, our bodies start to change more rapidly again until, inevitably, they stop working altogether and we die.

Humans are the only animals to give birth to a baby that remains helpless for so long. It takes about eight months before a baby can sit up without being supported and begins trying to feed itself. At about a year old, a baby usually begins to take its first tottering steps.

Humans also have a longer period of dependency than any other animal. Rabbits are capable of breeding just four months after they are born, and horses are mature when they are two years old. Only animals with large brains and complex lives have a childhood that even begins to approach the length of our own. Our extended childhood has almost certainly evolved to give us enough time, under the care and guidance of our parents, to learn all the complex information, language and skills that the human lifestyle requires.

Growing bigger, growing older

All living things are able to grow using the raw materials provided by food. Although their foods are totally different, the ways in which animals and plants grow are similar. To get bigger, all living things produce more cells. They change part of their food into material for new cells. These new cells are produced when those that are already present divide into two. The faster this cell division occurs, the faster a plant or animal will grow.

As a baby grows into a child and then into an adult, this multiplication of cells occurs. Most of the organs of the body are made of cells that can divide and increase in number and grow.

Animals grow at different rates at different times of their lives. A human grows fastest as a baby. The rate slows down after that, except for a growth spurt during puberty. Different parts of the body also grow at different rates. A baby's head grows more slowly than its legs and body after it is born.

All of these changes in growth are under careful control so that the final shape and size of the growing plant or animal is as it should be. Growth is often controlled by chemical messengers, or hormones. In humans the growth hormone is produced by the pituitary gland, a tiny outgrowth at the base of the front part of the brain. Growth is affected by other hormones as well, though, including those produced by the thyroid and pancreas. Plant hormones are different from those found in animals.

The human body continues to grow until we are about 18 or 20. Our mental abilities are usually thought to be at their best between the ages of 20 and 30, although most of us continue to be mentally active until we are very old.

The ultimate size of a human being, or any other living organism, can be affected by environmental conditions, such as the consistency and quality of food. It is also affected by heredity – the size of the parents, grandparents and other members of either generation.

See Chapter 4 for information on the differences in people's heights.

Technical terms

Grow, growth, egg, tall, taller, tallest, short, shorter, shortest, long, longer, longest, metre, centimetre, standard measurement, span.

1 GENERIC SHEET

Growing and changing

Growth

LESSON PLAN

Science objective (Unit 1A)
- To know that the term 'animal' includes humans.
- To know that all animals, including humans, grow and change as they get older.

Resources

- Height measuring charts
- Tape measures
- Items for measuring non-standard units
- Pieces of card, large sheets of paper and a marker pen
- Generic sheet 1 (page 36)
- Activity sheets 1–3 (pages 39–41)

Starting points: *whole class*

Tell the children that there are many different types of animal that live on the Earth. There are birds, reptiles (such as snakes), fish, mammals (such as lions), insects and amphibians (such as frogs). Explain that people are also animals and they are called humans. At this stage there is no need to go into great depth but simply to introduce the words.

Discuss what we mean by growing. Use Generic sheet 1 to remind the children how all animals grow and change. Talk about the animals in the top picture and how they have changed as they got older. Did they just get bigger? In what other ways might they have changed? Think about what food they eat when young and when they are older, the development of teeth, their behavioural changes as they get older, their fitness and so on. Next, look at the middle picture and talk about how these animals have changed as they have grown. They have done more than just get bigger; they have completely changed their appearance at some stage. Finally, look at the bottom picture and talk about how we change from a baby, developing teeth, starting to crawl, then walking and becoming young children at school, and so on.

Let everyone record their height on the height chart. Non-standard measurements could be used, as long as the same measuring device is used throughout. Then write each child's name and exact age in years and months on the chart. Before the children examine the chart, ask them whether they think the oldest child in the class will be the tallest. Will the youngest child be the smallest? (Be aware of any children who may be sensitive about their height and deal with it in a positive way, such as suggesting how short and tall people have advantages in many ways.)

Talk about how, as we grow, we get older. Is it anyone's birthday today? How can we tell people are getting older? Agree it is because their bodies change with age. Look at Generic sheet 1. Talk about how all the animals are shown in various stages of growing taller and growing older.

Group activities

Activity sheet 1
This sheet asks the children to identify the age four people appear to be and then put them in order from youngest to oldest.

Activity sheet 2
This sheet asks the children to identify the ages of six people and use the words in the word box to label them.

Activity sheet 3
This sheet is for the more able children. They have to identify six people, adults and children, from their ages. They are then asked to draw some of the activities that a baby and a six year-old girl might do.

Plenary session

Discuss how people change as they get older. Emphasise the fact that we have all grown from babyhood. Even the largest person we know began life as a tiny baby (or a tiny egg the size of a full stop inside the mother's body).

Ideas for support

Display the children's outlines made in a previous lesson arranged in order of increasing height to show the size variation in height of children of approximately the same age and the fact that we grow at different rates. Also display the height charts to emphasise these points.

Ideas for extension

Invite a baby brother or sister of one of the children to visit the classroom with his or her mother. Take measurements of the baby and compare these measurements with those of an older sibling.

Choose photographs of the children now and ask them to paint or draw what they think they will look like in ten years' time.

Make a display of clothes to show how we can measure rates of growth. As well as clothes and shoes of different sizes you could display baby mittens, a toddler's gloves and then those of a teenager and adult.

Devise a questionnaire for the children to take home for parents or carers to fill in, to record milestones in the children's growth.

Measure the growth of hair or fingernails at weekly intervals for a month or six weeks.

Linked ICT activities

Using the Internet, show the children how we can find information using the computer. Search for websites that show the different animals and their young. Give the children a list of the different animals and their young you would like them to find, such as sheep and lamb, and hen and chicken. Show them how to use a simple search engine, such as Google, to find the different animals on the websites. Look for photographs that show the animals at different stages of growth; for example, tadpole to frog. Print out the pictures and ask the children to sequence them to show the different stages of growth for the different animals.

Ask the children to bring pictures from home of themselves as babies. Using the digital camera, let them take photographs of each other to print out and display alongside the picture of themselves as babies.

Name _____

Growing

ACTIVITY SHEET 1

Cut out the pictures below and put them in order of growing older.

PHOTOCOPIABLE

CURRICULUM FOCUS • OURSELVES   39

Name _____

Growing

ACTIVITY SHEET 2

Look at the pictures of people below. Choose from the different ages in the box and write them under the pictures.

| Aged 2 | Aged 6 | Aged 12 | Aged 20 |
| Aged 50 | Aged 70 |

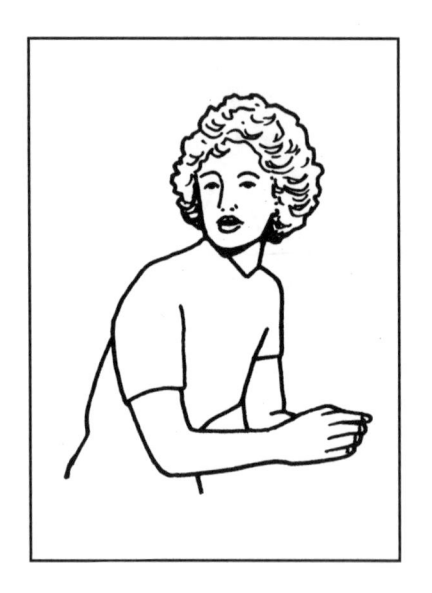

_____ _____ _____

_____ _____ _____

40   CURRICULUM FOCUS • OURSELVES

PHOTOCOPIABLE

Name _____

Growing

3 ACTIVITY SHEET

As we grow, we get bigger. It takes time to grow. Look at these people. Write the people's names under their pictures.

- Judith is 6 months old.
- Annabel is 6 years old.
- Michael is 18 years old.
- Iqbal is 2 years old.
- Ben is 12 years old.
- Mrs Peters is 40 years old.

On the back of the sheet, draw some of the things that Judith and Annabel might do.

PHOTOCOPIABLE

CURRICULUM FOCUS • OURSELVES 41

Chapter 4

Differences

TEACHERS' NOTES

We are all different

Individuals within any species – plant or animal – are all slightly different from each other. There are more than six billion people living on Earth and, although we all have the same basic features, no two people are exactly alike.

Many of the small variations that exist between people today, such as differences in skin colour, type of hair, the number of sweat glands in the skin and differences in blood groups, arose as bands of people spread throughout the world from East Africa where they first evolved and had to adapt to different climates.

We inherit characteristics from our parents, sometimes in a different form and sometimes altered by influences such as diet, activity, environment and health. The limit to a person's height, for example, is inherited, yet children may grow taller than their parents because of a more nutritious diet or a better exercise regime. Children may inherit a tendency to have good, strong teeth, but if they have a diet high in sugar and sticky foods, or fail to clean their teeth properly, tooth decay could occur anyway.

The particular combination of traits a person inherits is due to chance. Nevertheless, we all share characteristics with our parents and ancestors. Such inherited characteristics are controlled by genetic instructions – genes – which are carried on chromosomes. Chromosomes are microscopically small, thread-like structures in the nucleus of every cell of the body. One set of genes comes from each parent during reproduction. Many of our features, including hair and eye colour, are determined at fertilisation, with one set of genes coming from our father and one from our mother.

The transfer of sets of genes from each parent during fertilisation produces most variation. However, sometimes a completely new variation occurs which can still be inherited. Such striking mutations are caused by a change in the chemistry of a gene or in the structure of a chromosome, and these constantly occur. Some mutations have only slight effects, but most are harmful or even lethal.

One example of a harmful mutation is haemophilia, an inherited blood disorder. It is caused by a mutation in a gene that affects the way the blood clots. The blood of haemophiliacs clots very slowly, so that they may bleed to death from minor injuries. Queen Victoria was born with a mutant gene for haemophilia and, although she did not have the disease herself, she passed the gene through the royal families of Europe.

To sum up, some variation is controlled by the environment and is not passed from one generation to the next. Some variation is controlled by genes and can be passed on from generation to generation. Much of the variation we see in people is a result of both the environment and genes. As a result, there are, broadly, two types of variation. Some characteristics, such as height, weight or intelligence, show a whole range of variation. This is called continuous variation, and it results from the actions of two or more genes, together with environmental factors. There are some other characteristics where there are clear-cut differences between individuals. For example, some people can roll their tongues in from the sides and others cannot; some people have ear lobes that hang freely and others lack such lobes. These are examples of what is called discontinuous variation, and they result from the actions of a single pair of genes.

Body measurements

In the case of height and build there is a tendency for the population to show continuous variation from one extreme to the other, with most people fairly close to the average of the population, and fewer and fewer people represented as one moves towards either of the two extremes. This is typical of the situation one would expect to find in a population where the variation is due to a number of causes, each of small effect.

Studies of twins suggest that the height of adults is largely determined by genetic factors, except where illness has actually deformed the skeleton. The difference in height between adult identical twins is rarely more than 2.5cm, even where the twins were brought up in different environments. The height of most other children, by contrast, appears to be much more subject to environmental factors, such as nutrition. Between 1900 and 1970 the average height of 11-year-olds increased by about 10cm. This change was partly ascribed to more favourable environmental circumstances.

The genetic factor in the determination of height seems to come into play at different stages during development. At birth it plays very little part, and there is no relationship between the height of a baby and its mother's height. By the age of three, genetic factors are operating, and the height is related to its final adult height. At puberty there is a spurt in height. In general, the later the onset of this sudden growth spurt, the greater the final height of the individual. What environmental improvements appear to be doing is, in the main, to accelerate growth, so that full adult height is being reached earlier. Puberty is being reached at a steadily younger age in both boys and girls and almost full adult height is being reached on average at about 18 years of age. At the beginning of the last century, only men in the most favoured social classes reached adult height at 18 years old.

One study of the inheritance of height compared fathers and sons. It showed that the sons of tall men tended to be tall, but not as tall as their fathers. Similarly, the sons of short men tended to be short, but not as short as their fathers. In each case the sons showed considerable variation in their heights, but the average tended to be halfway towards the average height of the general population. Again, this regression is what one would expect with a characteristic controlled by several genes.

Hands

By the time we are ten years old, one side of our brain is usually dominant for certain functions. The left side of the brain controls the right side of the body, and the right side of the brain controls the left side of the body. This reversal is due to the fact that nerve fibres cross over on their way in and out of the brain. For direct physical acts, like writing, one side of the brain is usually in charge; if you are right-handed, then the left side of the brain is in control. Some people are 'ambidextrous' – they can use either hand to do a task. Other people are 'mixed handed' – they do different tasks with different hands.

Skin and fingerprints

Human skin comes in a variety of colours. Skin colouring depends on pigments, skin thickness and its blood supply. The key pigment is melanin, which ranges in colour from yellow to black. The cells that produce melanin are between the outer and inner layers of the skin. The outer layer, the epidermis, is made up of dead cells while the inner layer, the dermis, contains blood vessels, oil and sweat glands, nerve cells and hair roots. Skin may be as thick as 5mm on the soles of the feet or as thin as 0.5mm over the eyes. The dermis and epidermis interlock by little cone-like bumps, called papillae, that go upward from the dermis and fit in corresponding hollows in the epidermis. The papillae are arranged in parallel rows that make swirling patterns. These are the lines you see in a fingerprint.

All skin prints – whether from the fingers, toes, palms or soles – can be divided into three general ridge patterns: arches (5 per cent of the population) loops (60 to 65 per cent) and whorls (30 to 35 per cent). In the arch pattern, ridges extend across the fingertip and rise slightly at the centre. The loop pattern has one or more ridges curving into a hairpin turn. Ridges in the whorl pattern create a spiral or circle in the end of the fingertip.

Each person's fingerprints are unique and so they are a good way to identify people. When a person touches an object, a small amount of sweat and oil from the skin surface is transferred to the object. The sweat and oil are in the pattern of the person's fingerprints. Powder or dust stick to the sweat and oil and make the fingerprint visible. Powder and dust have been used since the late 1800s to reveal fingerprints, but they do not work on surfaces such as cloth and paper. Newer methods of revealing fingerprints make use of lasers, the light from which cause the oil and sweat to shine with a yellow colour so that the fingerprint can be photographed.

Eye and hair colour

Many of our features, including hair and eye colour, are determined at fertilisation, with one set of genes coming from our father and one from our mother. If, at fertilisation, two genes for blonde hair came together, then we ourselves would be blonde. Of course, the genes could carry different instructions, for instance one for blonde hair and one for dark brown hair. The result is not striped hair or hair of an intermediate colour. What usually happens is that one gene will be dominant over the other and will control the character. The other gene is said to be recessive. As it happens, dark brown hair is dominant over blonde hair, so that if we receive a blonde hair gene and a dark brown hair gene, our hair will be dark brown. The gene for brown eyes is similarly dominant over the gene for blue eyes, which explains why the vast majority of the world's people have brown eyes. Blue eyes is a weaker, or recessive, hereditary trait.

We cannot always tell what sort of genes a person possesses, simply by looking at him or her. A brown-eyed person could, for example, have two genes for brown eyes or one dominant gene for brown eyes and one recessive gene for blue eyes. In the latter case, only in the creation of subsequent generations will two blue-eyed genes come together so that an offspring with blue eyes is born.

The actual colour of the eyes comes from the iris. Whether the iris is brown, blue or green depends on a pigment called melanin, which also determines hair and skin colour. Someone with a large amount of melanin will have brown or hazel eyes; a person with less melanin will have blue or light green eyes.

In a few instances, the eyes are neither brown, blue or green but pink. This is due to albinism, a rare genetic disorder that inhibits the production of melanin. Victims of albinism often have skin and hair that are snowy white. At birth their eyes are almost transparent, although they later darken a little. Victims of albinism suffer a number of eye problems, including intolerance to bright lights. Fortunately severe albinism affects only about one person in 20,000.

Each hair grows from its own little hollow, or follicle, in the skin. Only the bottom part of the hair in the follicle is alive, and new cells are produced here that push up the old dead ones, so that the hair lengthens. The shape of the follicle determines the type of hair you have. Wavy hair grows from oval-shaped follicles: straight hair from round ones; and curly hair from flat ones.

Whether the outside temperature is hot or cold, the temperature inside our bodies stays at a constant 37°C, unless we are ill. Skin helps us to maintain this constant temperature, partly with the help of the three million or so sweat glands in our skin. When we are hot, the blood vessels under the skin dilate to increase the blood flow to the surface, making the skin look redder. Then these sweat glands release droplets of sweat, which make the surface of the skin wet. The sweat evaporates, turning into water vapour, which escapes into the air. To do this it uses energy and takes heat from your skin, so cooling it down. When we are cold, the tiny blood vessels threaded through the skin shut down to prevent the warm blood being cooled.

Technical terms
Hand, finger, thumb, fingerprint, skin, hair, colour, body, ear, eye, measurement, height, weight, tall, short.

We are all different

Science objective (Unit 1A)
- To understand that there are differences between humans.

Resources
- Pictures of groups of people
- Hand mirrors
- Tape measures
- Bathroom scales
- Activity sheets 1–3 (pages 47–49)

Starting points: *whole class*

Show the children pictures of different groups of people. Ask them to tell you all the differences they can see between them – height, body shape, male, female, skin colour, facial hair, hair type, clothes and so on.

Group the children's names into two sets – boys and girls. Explain that although humans are all built in the same way, there are also many differences between individuals – differences in appearance, likes and dislikes, hobbies and interests, musical tastes. Can the children suggest ways in which they are different from their friends or other people in their own family?

Refer to the height chart made in the previous lesson. Ask the children whether they think other body measurements will be different. Does everyone have the same size feet? Handspan? Head?

Write on the board 'Feet', 'Handspan' and 'Head'. Send the children off to work in pairs to measure these parts of each other's body and record their findings.

Back as a class, ask them if they found out anything that surprised them.

Now compile a table of their likes and dislikes. This could include such things as:
- food I like/dislike;
- drink I like/dislike;
- sport I like/dislike;
- music I like/dislike;
- animals I like/dislike.

Discuss the results. Are there differences in results for each like or dislike? Do any two children have exactly the same results?

Group activities

Activity sheet 1
This sheet concentrates mainly on gender differences and physical features and measurements.

Activity sheet 2
This sheet is slightly more difficult in that, as well as recording differences in gender, and physical features and measurements in chart form there are questions to answer about the findings.

Activity sheet 3
This sheet is for the more able children and it provides them with the opportunity to detail more of their characteristics and likes and dislikes.

Plenary session

Discuss the results of the whole-class activity and the differentiated activity sheets. Can the children find anyone who has exactly the same build and features and likes and dislikes as themselves? Stress that although we are all similar in many ways there is no one else in the world exactly like each one of us.

Ideas for support

Help with spelling the various likes and dislikes if necessary, and check that the children have recorded their answers correctly. The children may also need help in measuring and weighing themselves. Use non-standard measurements for height where it is thought appropriate.

Display some of the photographs of groups of people and label the more obvious differences such as 'tall', 'short', 'fat', 'thin', 'curly hair', 'straight hair' and so on. Display some of the children's tables of likes and dislikes.

Ideas for extension

Compare sporting or athletic prowess – for example, in running, jumping, catching a ball and kicking a ball.

Linked ICT activities

Talk to the children about all the different foods they like to eat. What do they like for breakfast? What is their favourite snack food? What is their favourite fruit? (Don't forget to include healthy foods within this choice.) Talk to the children about how they can record their favourite foods on the computer. Show them the program 'Pick a Picture' (Granada Learning, Semerc). Explain that they can choose their favourite foods and record them in this program. Show them how to enter the information into their own datafile using the pictures to help them. Then show them how to save the information. Once they have entered their information, show them how to look through the other files to see what their friends have chosen as their favourite food.

Name _____

We are different

ACTIVITY SHEET 1

Complete the chart below to show the differences between you and a friend.

Picture of me	Picture of my friend
Name _____	Name _____
Put a ✔	Put a ✔
Boy ☐ Girl ☐	Boy ☐ Girl ☐
Eyes: blue ☐ brown ☐ green ☐ grey ☐	Eyes: blue ☐ brown ☐ green ☐ grey ☐
Hair: black ☐ brown ☐ blonde ☐ red ☐	Hair: black ☐ brown ☐ blonde ☐ red ☐
I am _____ centimetres tall. I weigh _____ kilograms. My shoes are size _____	I am _____ centimetres tall. I weigh _____ kilograms. My shoes are size _____

PHOTOCOPIABLE

CURRICULUM FOCUS • OURSELVES

Name _____

We are different

ACTIVITY SHEET 2

Complete the chart below to show the differences between you and two other people.

	Name _____	Name _____	Name _____
Boy/girl			
Eye colour			
Hair colour			
Height			
Weight			
Shoe size			
Handspan			

Now answer the following questions.

Does everyone have the same hair colour? _____

Who is the tallest? _____

Who has the smallest feet? _____

Who has the biggest handspan? _____

48 CURRICULUM FOCUS • OURSELVES

PHOTOCOPIABLE

Name _____

We are different

ACTIVITY SHEET 3

Complete the chart below to show the differences and similarities between everyone in your class. You will need to ask questions and keep a record of all the answers.

Number of boys ☐

Number of girls ☐

Most favourite food
_____

Most favourite game
_____

Most favourite animal
_____

Most favourite music
_____

Most favourite book
_____

Number of people with blue eyes ☐

Number of people with brown eyes ☐

Number of people with green eyes ☐

Number of people with grey eyes ☐

Number of people with red hair ☐

Number of people with blonde hair ☐

Number of people with brown hair ☐

Number of people with black hair ☐

The most common shoe size ☐

The most common handspan ☐

The tallest person ☐

The shortest person ☐

Think of more questions to ask people to find out how we are all different. Present your findings in a chart. You could include adults in your research.

PHOTOCOPIABLE

CURRICULUM FOCUS • OURSELVES

Movement

TEACHERS' NOTES

Movement on land

All animals can move some part of themselves and most can move their entire body. This enables them to move from place to place, to find shelter, to escape their enemies, to seek a mate or to search for food. In all but the simplest animals, muscles provide the power that enables animals to move. The way an animal moves depends on its shape, size, surroundings and its type of food. Herbivores can move at a leisurely pace in search of food because plants cannot run away. But when a herbivore is attacked by a fast-moving carnivore, it must either stand and fight or run for its life.

On land, the slowest animals move by creeping or crawling, and keeping a large part of their body on the ground. Slugs and snails, for example, creep over the ground on a flat, muscular foot that works like a sucker. The muscles of the foot contract in waves that run from the front to the rear of the animal. The foot is always in contact with the ground, which limits the animal's speed. Both slugs and snails secrete a mucus trail which helps them to move over rough surfaces.

Although the largest land animals have four legs, many of the smallest have six, eight or even more legs. All of these legs need to be carefully coordinated when the animal walks or runs. A millipede, for example, has four legs on each of the many segments of its body. These legs move in waves, thus preventing the legs of one segment from colliding with those of the next.

Most mammals have limbs powerful enough to lift the animal's belly clear of the ground. A cat walks permanently on tiptoe. It can also jump, climb and run. Soft pads under its toes act as cushions, allowing it to move very quietly when stalking prey. A rabbit moves mainly by jumping and running and it can leap long distances to escape a predator. When it is at rest, its long hind legs are folded into a Z-shape and the whole hind foot rests on the ground. As the rabbit leaps, powerful muscles straighten its hind legs.

Like a cat, a horse also walks on tiptoe but, unlike a cat's foot, a horse's foot consists of a very large toe protected by a hoof. This single toe corresponds to the middle toe of a five toed animal. When walking, a horse normally has three feet on the ground acting as a tripod that supports the animal's weight while it moves the fourth foot. When it trots, a horse has two feet on the ground while the two diagonally opposite feet are moving. When it gallops, for an instant all four of a horse's feet leave the ground. The horse's long, flexible backbone helps to give the animal a big stride.

Humans are one of the few animals to walk upright for much of their life. This has meant changes to our muscles and bones, especially those of the foot and back. Some changes are not complete, which is why people can have trouble with their backs, hips and feet as they get older. Changes in the pelvis to allow for an upright gait mean birth is more difficult for humans than for other animals. Babies have to turn a corner to get out of the womb, instead of having a straightforward slide helped by gravity.

Life in water

Life began in the water, and water is still the natural habitat for a vast range of animal life, from tiny single-celled creatures to the blue whale, the largest animal that has ever lived. Water is much denser than air and helps to support the animal's body. On the other hand, the resistance, or friction, of water also slows an animal down, which is why many aquatic animals have a slippery surface and a streamlined body shape.

Almost all fish swim by sweeping their muscular tail from side to side. As the tail fin is swept from side to side it pushes backwards against the water, and this pushes the fish forwards. The animal maintains a straight course by using its other fins as rudders and stabilisers. Fish have a streamlined shape and many are made weightless in water by an air-filled space called a swim bladder.

Whales, porpoises and dolphins are the only mammals that spend their whole lives in water. Unlike seals they do not even return to land to breed. Whales, porpoises and dolphins swim using a horizontal tail fin which sweeps up and down, to push the body forwards, and not from side to side like a fish's tail. Unlike fish which have gills, whales, porpoises and dolphins have lungs and they have to come to the surface from time to time to breathe air.

Flight

Bats, birds and some insects can defy the force of gravity and take to the air and remain airborne for long periods. A few other animals can glide for short distances on fins or flaps of skin. Either way, the animal has to have a large surface area to push against the air.

A bird's wings have two functions. They provide a force called lift, which overcomes the force of gravity. They also flap to drive the bird forward through the air. The wings are powered by large chest muscles attached to a projection on the breast bone, called the keel.

In cross-section a bird's wing has a curved shape, called an aerofoil. As an aerofoil moves through the air its shape forces the air to move faster across the upper surface than across its underside. Fast moving air has a lower pressure than slower moving air. As a result, a moving wing has a low pressure air stream above it and a higher pressure air stream under it. The difference between these two pressures is an upward force – called lift. A bird stays in the air if lift equals or is greater than the weight of the body. Small birds, such as sparrows, fly almost entirely by flapping their wings. Some larger birds, such as eagles or buzzards, often save energy by gliding or soaring. To reduce their weight, many of the bones in a bird's body are hollow.

Bones and skeletons

Human beings have an internal skeleton made up of more than 200 bones (usually 206). The skeleton supports and protects the body and allows free movement. At the same time, it allows the body to grow normally.

The bones in the skeleton have a number of functions. They protect delicate organs. The heart and lungs, for example, are protected by a bony framework (the chest) formed by the ribs. The backbone protects the spinal cord, while the brain is protected by the box of bone we call the skull. Bones also give shape to the body, hold it upright and provide an attachment for muscles. Some bones store minerals and manufacture red blood cells. Different parts of the body need to move in different ways and this is brought about with the help of joints. A joint is a place where two or more bones meet. Some joints, such as the knee joint, allow movement in one direction only. This is called a hinge joint. A ball-and-socket joint, as in the joint between the thighbone and hip and upper arm bone and shoulder, can move in all directions. There are some places in the body where bones meet but there is no movement at all, as in the bones of the skull and pelvis. These are called immovable joints.

Muscles and movement

Movement of the body is brought about by muscles. There are more than 400 different muscles in the human body. The ends of muscles are attached to bones by tough cords called tendons. The tendons are very prominent behind the knees and on the backs of the hands and tops of the feet. There is also one very large tendon in the back of each ankle, known as the Achilles tendon. When a muscle pulls on a tendon, the bone it is attached to moves at a joint.

The muscles of the upper arm provide a good illustration of how muscles work. There are two main muscles in the upper arm, the biceps at the front of the arm and the triceps at the back. If you clench your fist and bend your elbow to raise the forearm, you will see (and feel) the biceps muscle changing shape. It becomes shorter and fatter (or contracts). At the same time, the triceps muscle on the back of the upper arm becomes longer and thinner, or relaxes. When you lower the forearm, the opposite happens.

Since muscles are flexible structures (the 'lean' of a joint of meat is muscle) they can only shorten or contract to pull bones. Muscles cannot push and so it always takes two muscles to move a bone. Wherever there is a muscle, there is another muscle that works against it.

Muscles always work in pairs. When someone smiles, one set of muscles pulls the mouth into the smile, while another set pulls the mouth back into its relaxed shape again. All muscle contraction needs energy and so uses up food and oxygen. Muscles are well supplied with blood vessels, to bring food and oxygen to them and to take away their waste products. Unless they are used regularly, muscles quickly become weak and tire easily.

Moving about

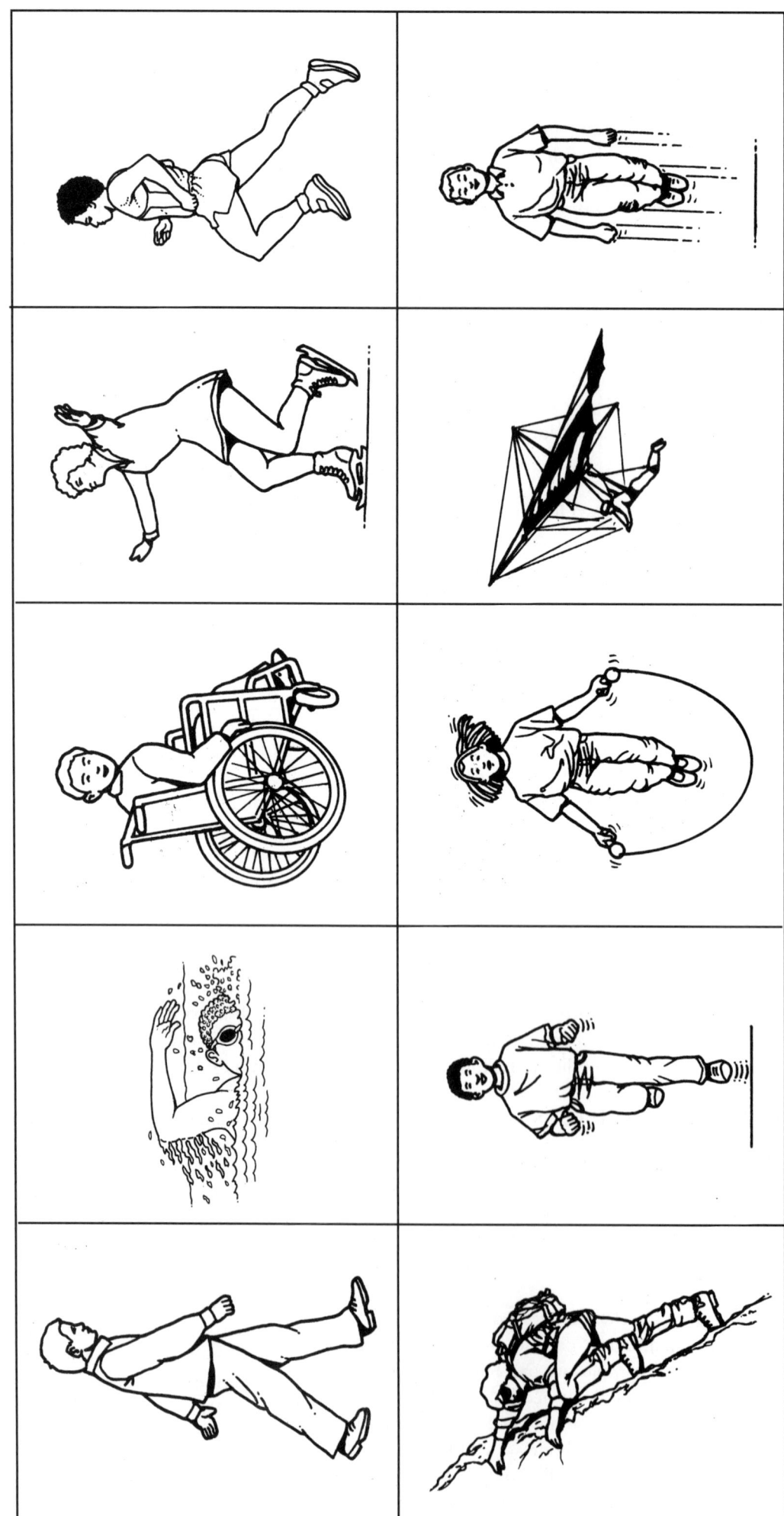

GENERIC SHEET 1

52 CURRICULUM FOCUS • OURSELVES

PHOTOCOPIABLE

Moving about

2 GENERIC SHEET

PHOTOCOPIABLE

CURRICULUM FOCUS • OURSELVES 53

LESSON PLAN

Moving about

Science objective (Unit 1A)
- That animals, including humans, move.

Resources
- Generic sheets 1 and 2 (pages 52 and 53)
- Activity sheet 1–3 (pages 56 to 58)

Starting points: *whole class*

Display an enlarged copy of Generic sheet 1. Ask the children to examine the pictures carefully. What are all the people in the pictures doing? Hopefully, the children will conclude that all the people are moving. Now ask them to name the different ways in which the people are moving – walking, swimming, running, jumping, hopping, flying and so on. Ask them to tell you in each case which parts of the body the people are using to make the movements.

Next display the pictures of the animals on Generic sheet 2. Discuss the different ways the animals are moving. Talk about the different movements and what we call them. We say that a spider 'crawls' but does it really crawl? Is the snake crawling or slithering? Ask the children to tell you in each case which parts of the body the animals are using to make the movements.

On the board write the headings 'walk', 'run', 'fly' and 'swim'. As you agree how each of the animals is moving, write its name under the correct heading.

Discuss with the children some different movements. Emphasise that some of our movements are very small, such as when we breathe in and out. Other movements are large when, for example, we run or jump. Point out that we mostly move around on two legs, unlike most other animals, some of which have many legs.

Group activities

Activity sheet 1
This sheet is aimed at children who can name the main methods by which animals move from place to place – chosen from a list.

Activity sheet 2
This sheet is aimed at children who can list the names of animals under the correct heading in the charts provided. They are then asked to think of more animals to add to the lists.

Activity sheet 3
This sheet is for the more able children. They have to draw up their own chart that shows how a variety of animals move, and then think of more animals to add to it.

Plenary session

Ask the children why we need to move in various ways. Describe, simply, how our bones and muscles help us to move. Ask the children to describe the ways in which animals move. Make a list of words which describe animal movements, such as 'crawl', 'hop', 'run', 'fly', 'gallop', 'trot', 'slide', 'swim', 'dive' and so on. Discuss why animals need to move from place to place including to find food, to escape enemies, to find shelter and to find a mate.

Ideas for support

Ask the children to name different ways of moving. Discuss where the joints and muscles are that allow these types of movement. How easy is it to walk without bending your legs? Will your legs bend forwards at the knee? What would happen if they did? Help the children to name and locate the main joints: hip, shoulder, knee, elbow, ankle, finger, toe and neck.

Ideas for extension

Use the pictures from the Generic sheets and differentiated worksheets and ask the children to divide them into sets according to whether the animals move mainly on land, in water or in the air.

Demonstrate how a string puppet works, to show how our muscles pull on our bones to produce movement.

Play 'Simon says' (for example, run on the spot, jump, skip, wave your arms and bend your knee). The children should obey the instructions only if told that 'Simon says' to do so.

Compare the strength of muscles in different parts of the body. Place bathroom scales vertically against the bottom of a wall. Each child lies at right angles to the wall and presses one foot against the scales, then the other. Now try the hands individually, and then a single finger from each hand. Which are the most powerful muscles?

Linked ICT activities

Talk to the children about how we can make things that are not living move. Show them a selection of toys that can move in different ways – a toy to pull or push, a wind up toy and a remote control toy. Tell the children that computers are used by companies that make things move. Ask them where they think they might find computers that may help something to move. Think about cars, aeroplanes, washing machines, sliding doors and so on. Ask the children how they think these objects move. Show them a programmable toy or a Roamer if you have one in school. Demonstrate how it is controlled to move forward and backward.

Talk about how we move around and how a programmable toy moves around. How are we different? Ask the children to work in pairs, taking it in turns to be a programmable toy. One child gives the other some simple directions around the classroom. Then they change places. How easy or difficult it was to give directions to control the other person?

Name _____

Moving about

ACTIVITY SHEET 1

Look at these animals. Underneath each one say how it is moving. Choose your answers from the word bank below.

WORD BANK

swim   walk   run   fly   crawl

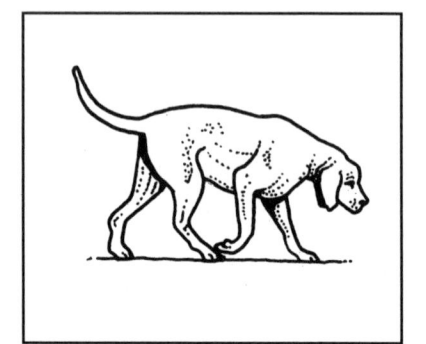

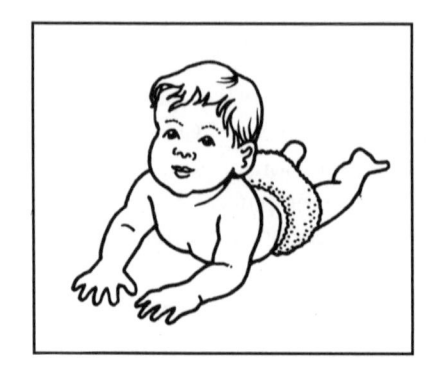

56 CURRICULUM FOCUS • OURSELVES

PHOTOCOPIABLE

Name _____

Moving about

ACTIVITY SHEET 2

Look at these animals. Decide how each one is moving and then write its name under the correct heading.

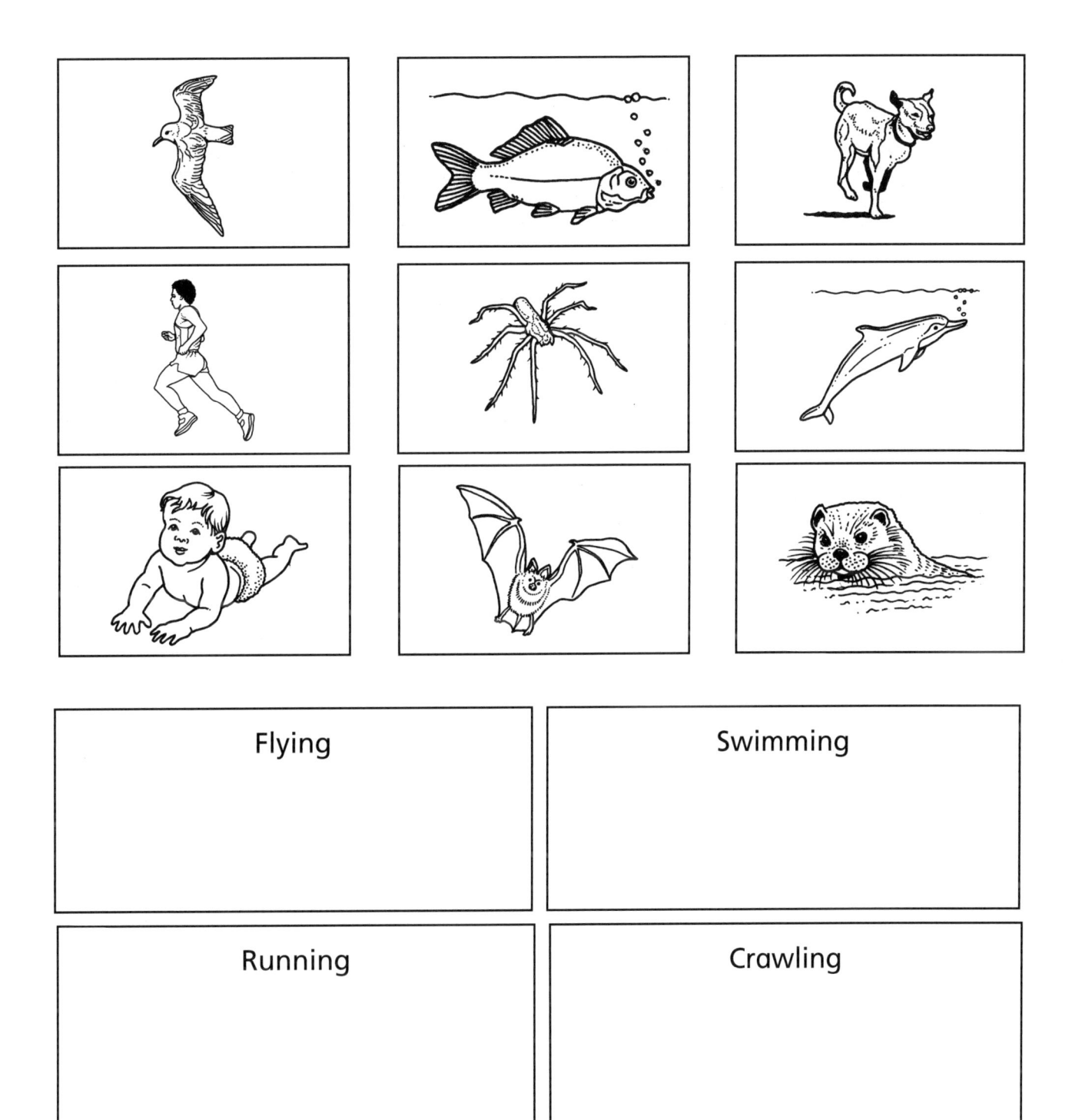

Flying	Swimming

Running	Crawling

Think of some more animals to add to the lists.

PHOTOCOPIABLE

CURRICULUM FOCUS • OURSELVES 57

Name _____

Moving about

ACTIVITY SHEET 3

Look at these animals. In the space below the pictures, draw up a chart that shows their names and how each of them is moving. Then think of some more animals to add to the chart.

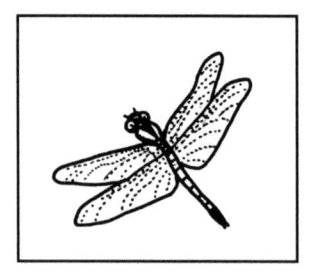

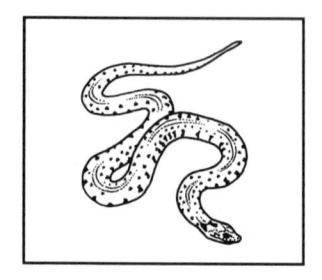

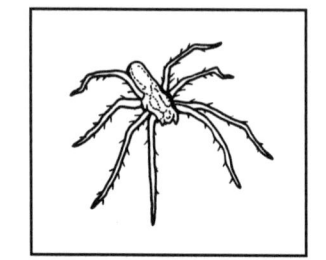

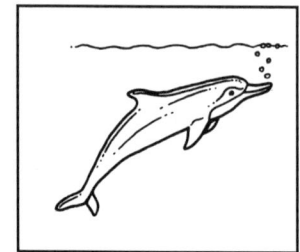

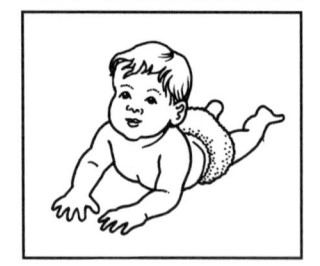

58 CURRICULUM FOCUS • OURSELVES

PHOTOCOPIABLE

Living and non-living

CHAPTER 6

TEACHERS' NOTES

Living things

Young children often find it difficult to decide whether an object is 'living' or 'alive'. Only by observing and experiencing a large number of examples of living and non-living objects can they begin to understand fully what it means to be 'living' or 'alive'. Even more experience is needed before they can distinguish between those objects which are living, those which are non-living, and those such as a piece of metal or rock, which have never been alive.

To help them decide what is alive, scientists group together the features that living things have in common:

- they have some kind of movement;
- they take in food from their surroundings;
- they take in oxygen from their surroundings;
- they excrete their waste products;
- they reproduce themselves;
- they grow;
- they are sensitive to their surroundings.

These, then, are the characteristics shared by all living things, apart from bacteria and viruses.

1 Movement

All living things are capable of some movement. Most animals move using legs, wings or fins. Plants mainly move by growing – for example, roots grow downwards away from the light or towards water, while shoots grow towards the light. Some single-celled plants do, however, actively swim around in fresh or sea water.

2 Feeding

All living things need food to provide energy and for growth. Animals obtain their food by eating plants, other animals, or the dead remains of plants and animals. Most plants make their own food, using sunlight energy to combine carbon dioxide gas and water to make sugars, in the process called photosynthesis.

3 Respiration

All living things need energy for movement, for growth and to work the various parts of the body. This energy is obtained by respiration, during which a number of chemical changes release energy from the food, usually by combining the food with oxygen.

4 Excretion

All living things produce waste substances as a result of the chemical reactions that take place in their cells. Carbon dioxide (a waste product of respiration), urine, water, and other chemicals may be excreted.

5 Reproduction

All living things reproduce, to replace organisms that die or are eaten, otherwise the species will become extinct. Some plants and a few simple animals can reproduce by splitting in two, or by the growth of parts which break off from the parent organism. This is asexual reproduction. Most animals are either male or female and reproduce sexually. The flowers of plants contain sexual organs which produce seeds that can grow into new plants.

6 Growth

All living things grow by a process of cell division. Animals grow until they reach a certain adult size, but most plants can grow continuously throughout their lives.

7 Sensitivity

All living things respond to changes in their environment. Many animals use sense organs such as eyes and ears, which are part of the nervous system, to find out about their surroundings. Humans, like all animals, respond to stimuli. They react positively to the features of their environment they like or need, and move away from stimuli they dislike or that are harmful. Although plants do not have specific sense organs, they are able to detect and respond to changes in such things as light, water and gravity.

Living and non-living

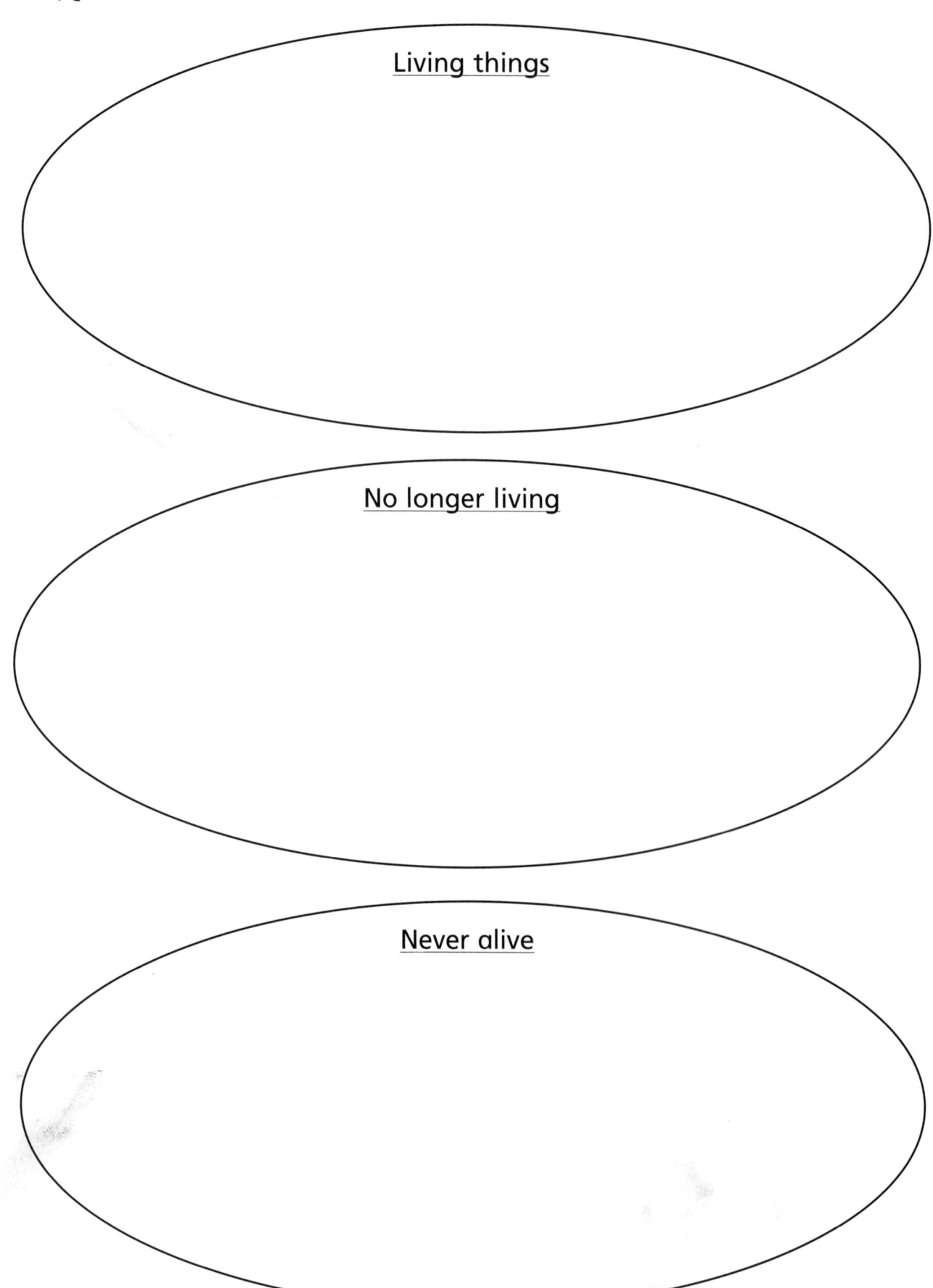

GENERIC SHEET 1

Living things

No longer living

Never alive

Living and non-living

Living and non-living

LESSON PLAN

> **Science objectives (Unit 1A)**
> - To know that animals, including humans, are living.
> - To know that living things need to eat and drink to stay alive.

Resources

- A collection of living and non-living things (stones, magnets, plants, books, food items, furniture, a living fish or gerbil, a snail or slug, a wooden spoon)
- A clockwork, or some other motorised, toy
- A television set
- Magazine pictures of living and non-living things
- Generic sheets 1 and 2 (pages 60 and 61)
- Actiivity sheets 1–3 (pages 64–66)

Starting points: *whole class*

Talk to the children about how we can tell whether or not something is alive. Ask what we would need to do, for example, to keep a pet dog, cat, rabbit or gerbil alive. Then move on to discuss the needs of, say, a human baby or an elderly person.

Begin by sorting the collection of objects into living and non-living things. Ask them to help you put them into two sets: things that are alive and things that are not alive. Agree that the living things are moving and to stay alive would need feeding. Agree that each, in their own way, breathes and they all have young.

When the children have sorted the objects into sets satisfactorily, ask them if they think a wooden spoon is alive. Agree it is not. Ask if they think it has ever been alive. Ask 'What does wood come from?' Explain that, in fact, a tree is alive because it grows, it feeds from the nutrients in the water that it takes up through its roots and it has young by creating and releasing seeds. But when it is cut down to make a wooden object it is no longer alive.

Explain that there are some things that have never been alive, such as rocks, stones and metal. These are all made up of materials that occur naturally on our planet but those materials have never fed or drunk, have never had young and don't move.

Go back to the pile of objects and sort the objects that are not alive into two piles, 'not alive' and 'have never been alive'. You should now have three sets of objects. Use an enlarged version of Generic sheet 1 to record the results.

Show an enlarged copy of Generic sheet 2. Discuss what each of the objects on it are. List them under the three headings.

Group activities

Activity sheet 1
This sheet requires the children to classify a group of objects into 'living' and 'non-living'.

Activity sheet 2
This sheet also requires the children to classify a group of objects into 'living' and 'non-living'. They are then asked to tick which of the objects have never been alive.

Activity sheet 3
This sheet is aimed at the more able children who may be able to classify a larger group of objects into 'living things', 'things that are no longer living' and 'things that have never been alive'.

Plenary session

Examine the results of the group work and ask the children to explain some of the decisions they have come to in arranging the pictures in sets or using the activity sheets. Some of them will have trouble identifying objects such as the loaf of bread. Make a point of explaining carefully the facts for each object. At this stage it will probably be sufficient for the children to know that living things need food and water, and that they grow, move, breathe and breed ('have babies' or reproduce).

Show the children a clockwork or some other motorised toy. Ask if, as it can move on its own, it is, therefore, alive.

Ideas for support

Young children often find it difficult to distinguish between things that are living and things such as a motorbike or television set, which have never been alive. It is best not to question them too hard to avoid confusion and to wait until they can work out the differences for themselves.

Make a display of representative examples of the three sets – 'living', 'no longer living' and 'never alive'.

Ideas for extension

More able children could construct a decision tree using simple questions that require 'Yes' or 'No' answers to clarify objects. Such questions might include:

- Does it move?
- Does it feed?
- Does it grow?
- Does it reproduce its own kind ('breed' or 'have babies')?

Linked ICT activities

Talk to the children about what we need to stay alive. Remind them about everything you have been discussing with them in previous chapters. Talk about exercise and how important that is to keep us healthy. Discuss healthy eating and the types of foods already mentioned that will help to keep us healthy. Talk about the things that plants, animals and humans need to live. List these on a flip chart or white board and leave the list pinned up in the classroom as a reference.

Show the children how to use a digital camera and tell them that they are going to work in pairs to take a picture of each other. Having taken the photograph, download the images to the computer and open them into a simple word processing program, such as 'Textease'. Show them how to add text to the pictures. Tell them that they are going to add different words to their photograph. The words should say what living things need to stay alive. They could use the word list agreed earlier.

Name _____

Living and non-living

ACTIVITY SHEET 1

Which of these things are living? Which are non-living?
Draw them in the boxes below.

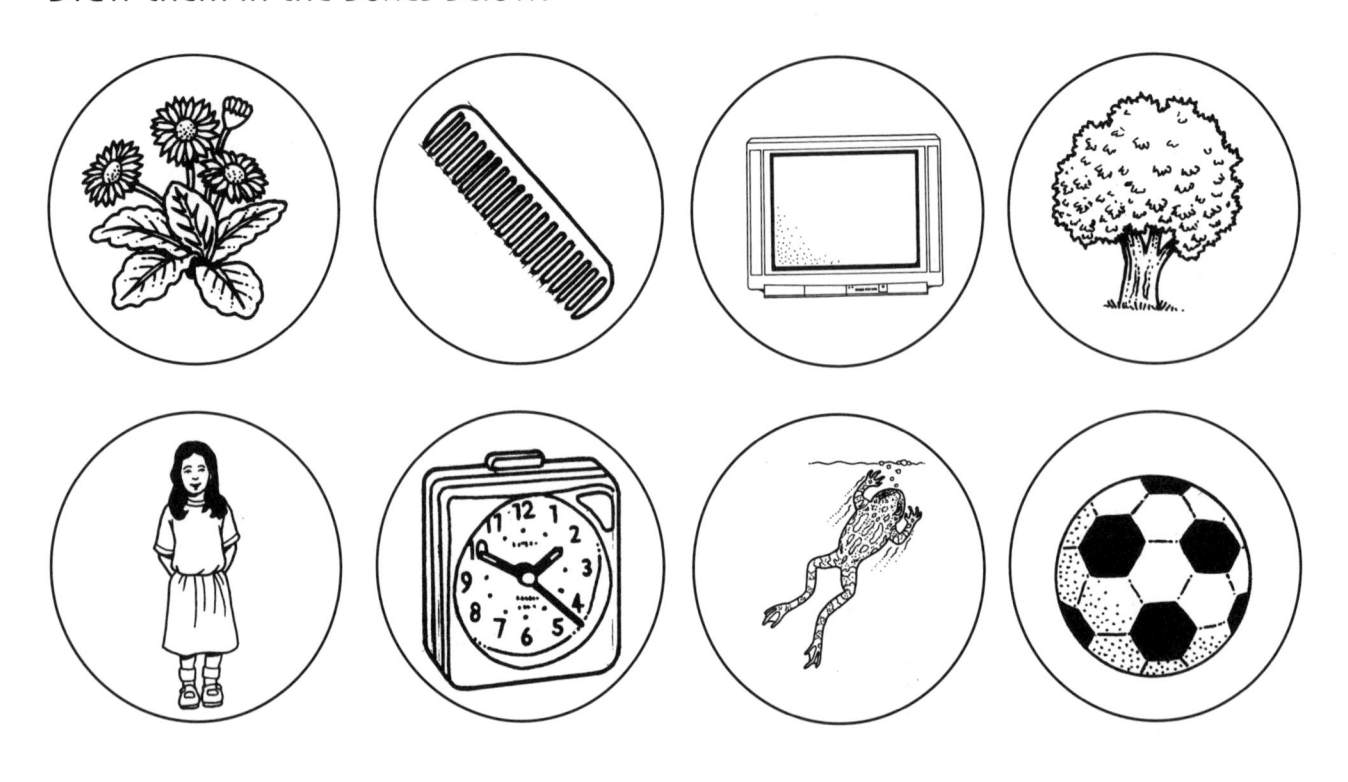

Living	Non-living

64 CURRICULUM FOCUS • OURSELVES

PHOTOCOPIABLE

Name _____

Living and non-living

ACTIVITY SHEET 2

Which of these things are living? Which are non-living?
Put a ✔ in the correct boxes below.

Living ☐	Living ☐	Living ☐	Living ☐
Not living ☐	Not living ☐	Not living ☐	Not living ☐
Never has lived ☐	Never has lived ☐	Never has lived ☐	Never has lived ☐

Living ☐	Living ☐	Living ☐	Living ☐
Not living ☐	Not living ☐	Not living ☐	Not living ☐
Never has lived ☐	Never has lived ☐	Never has lived ☐	Never has lived ☐

Living ☐	Living ☐	Living ☐	Living ☐
Not living ☐	Not living ☐	Not living ☐	Not living ☐
Never has lived ☐	Never has lived ☐	Never has lived ☐	Never has lived ☐

PHOTOCOPIABLE

CURRICULUM FOCUS • OURSELVES

Name _____

Living and non-living

3 ACTIVITY SHEET

Draw up a chart to show which of these things are living, non-living and have never been alive?

66 CURRICULUM FOCUS • OURSELVES

PHOTOCOPIABLE

Food and drink

TEACHERS' NOTES

A balanced diet

Food supplies us with energy and it is important to remember that all this energy comes either directly from plants or from animals that feed on plants. The plants in turn obtain their energy from sunlight. We also need food to enable us to grow, to repair damaged parts of our bodies, and to keep us warm and healthy. Eating a varied and balanced diet containing proteins, carbohydrates, fats, vitamins and mineral salts, together with adequate water and fibre or roughage, best fulfils these functions. Fibre or roughage aids the movement of the food through the digestive system and so prevents constipation and possibly also heart disease and bowel cancer.

How much energy an individual needs depends upon his or her physical size, level of activity and rate of growth. If a person regularly eats food containing more energy than is needed, then the extra food is stored in the body as fat. One in three adults is overweight or obese, and obesity in children is a growing problem in the developed countries of the world.

Weight for weight, fatty foods contain most energy, but many of us eat excessive amounts of starchy or sugary carbohydrate foods, such as cakes, biscuits and sweets, all of which have a high energy content. The latter foods are also important agents in the formation of the mouth acids that lead to tooth decay.

Digestion

Food must be changed inside the body before it can be used. The nutrients must dissolve before they can be passed through the gut wall and be carried around the body in the blood. Many of the nutrients are inside the cells of the pieces of plants and animals that make up our food. Our bodies must break open the cells to get at the nutrients. Mineral salts and most vitamins dissolve in water (or blood), but the very large molecules of proteins, carbohydrates and fats do not dissolve. To make these nutrients dissolve, the body has to break their molecules into smaller ones. This breakdown of large food molecules into smaller ones is called digestion.

Food is digested inside the gut, or alimentary canal, by chemicals called enzymes. The gut is a tube about eight metres long. It is coiled inside the abdomen. Each part of the alimentary canal has a different job to do. The journey from the mouth, where the food is crushed and chewed by the teeth so that it is easier to swallow, to the anus from where the undigested food is voided, is slow and may take 36 hours or more, depending on the nature of the food.

The kinds of foods we eat

There are various ways of grouping foods, including separating them into those which came from plants and those which came from animals, or those which are 'healthy' and those which are 'unhealthy'. More recently, we have had the separation of foods into 'organic' and 'non-organic'.

Scientifically it should be remembered that there are no good or bad foods, only bad diets. All the food we eat falls into a few basic categories, and it is important for our health and well-being that we have a diet that contains a balance of these food categories.

Carbohydrates such as sugars and starches release energy when they are digested and this energy can be used by the body cells. Carbohydrates are found in bread, cakes, pasta, potatoes, rice and jam, amongst other things. If you eat more carbohydrates than you need for your body's energy requirements, the surplus is stored as fat.

Proteins are found in eggs, meat, fish, dairy products, cereals and beans and peas. During digestion, proteins are broken down into small units called amino acids. These are then rearranged in the human body to form new proteins that are used to build cells, tissues and organs. Since proteins form part of every cell in the human body they are essential for growth.

Fats can produce twice as much energy as an equivalent weight of carbohydrate, but if the energy is not used immediately then the fat is stored under the skin until it is needed. About a quarter of the energy we use each day comes from fat. Sources of fat include butter, nuts, fatty meat, cream, vegetable oil and, of course, fried foods.

Mineral salts or 'minerals' describes a whole collection of chemicals that are essential in tiny quantities for good health. Calcium and phosphorus salts, for example, are needed to build healthy bones and teeth, while sodium and potassium salts are needed to keep nerves functioning properly. Iron salts are important for the formation of healthy blood cells. Mineral salts are found in small amounts in most foods, while fresh fruits and vegetables are good sources of many of these nutrients.

Vitamins are essential for health but, again, are only needed in tiny quantities. About 12 vitamins, known by the letters of the alphabet, are essential for health. There are small amounts of vitamins in most foods, and fresh fruits and vegetables are good sources of many vitamins. Vitamin C, needed for healthy teeth, gums and skin, is found mainly in fresh fruits and green vegetables, while vitamin D, needed for strong bones and teeth, can be made by the skin using the energy of sunlight. Vitamin D is also found in margarine, eggs and fish oils.

Fibre or roughage Many foods contain parts that the body either cannot use or does not want. Fruits, vegetables, cereals, peas, beans, brown rice and wholemeal bread, contain a lot of indigestible fibre. Fibre absorbs water as it travels through the digestive system and helps push waste food out of the body as faeces. If food takes too long to pass through the intestines it can cause constipation and possibly diseases such as bowel cancer and heart disease.

In general, to achieve a balanced diet, we should eat more fruit, vegetables and cereals, and more low fat sources of protein such as chicken, fish and beans. We should eat fewer fried foods, crisps, butter, sweets, jams and cakes, and less factory processed food, since the latter often contains preservatives and excessive amounts of sugar and salt. Finally, it should also be remembered that the body needs water to replace that lost during breathing, sweating and excretion.

Food and drink

Food and drink

LESSON PLAN

Science objectives (Unit 2A)
- To know that there are many different foods.
- To know that we eat different kinds of food.
- To know that humans need water and food to stay alive.

Resources
- Pictures of as many different foods as possible
- Generic sheet 1 (page 69)
- Activity sheets 1–3 (pages 72–74)

Starting points: *whole class*

Talk about why we eat food. When do we feel hungry? When do we feel thirsty? Ask the children to tell you what their favourite foods and drinks are. In carrying out this survey, divide foods up into the categories: meat, fish, vegetables, fruits, bread and puddings. Record the results on the board in the form of a chart.

Ask the children if they know where our food comes from. Children rarely think about where food comes from and how it is produced, so they will probably say 'the shops'. Help them to understand that all our food was originally grown in the form of a plant or animal. Examine the chart of favourite foods constructed earlier. Discuss whether each item came originally from plants or animals.

Show the children the pictures of foods on Generic sheet 1. Challenge them to identify whether they are plant or animal or neither (as in the case of water). Talk about whether the food has to be cooked or can be eaten as it is.

Now go on to talk about which foods are good for us and which are not so good. Tell the children that scientists are still making new discoveries every day about food and so we might not know everything about foods for sure. But say that we have a good idea of what is good for us. By 'good for us' explain that some foods give us healthy bodies, and so we have lots of energy, but others are not so good for us and can cause our bodies problems.

Be aware that young children have little or no say or control over what they are given to eat at home. Therefore, when discussing food and diets, take care that they do not feel that you disapprove of their dietary habits.

Talk through each of the foods pictured on the generic sheet and tell the children which are good for them and which are not so good for them if eaten in large amounts or too often.

Now tell them that they are going to do an activity in which they have to choose a healthy two course meal.

Group activities

Activity sheet 1
This sheet requires the children to create a healthy main meal and a dessert from the pictured ingredients.

Activity sheet 2
This sheet asks the children to devise and write down a healthy menu from a list of ingredients.

Activity sheet 3
This sheet is for the more able children. They are asked to devise their favourite menu from a list of ingredients. They are then asked to devise a menu for a healthy meal.

Plenary session

Ask the children what is the longest gap between meals. Use this opportunity to emphasise the importance of starting the day with a good breakfast. (As some children may start the day with little or no breakfast, this should be handled tactfully.) Discuss what might constitute a good breakfast.

Talk about their choice of menus. Display them. Did any of the children who did Activity sheet 3 have a 'good for you' meal as their favourite?

Ideas for support

Display the class chart of favourite foods and some of the food sets the children have devised with their pictures. Use these to emphasise the fact that there is no one 'ideal' meal and that as long as a meal contains a variety of foods, it is good for you. Stress that the occasional meal that is not well balanced does no harm. Remember that it is also important that the children drink lots of water and not just sweet or fizzy drinks.

Ideas for extension

Visit a food shop or supermarket and examine the different foods available, where they come from (country as well as plant/animal), and how they are kept fresh.

Make a collection of clean food containers – jars, packets, cans and other containers. Compile a chart showing whether the foods came from plants or animals and a map showing their country of origin.

Linked ICT activities

Give the children a printed sheet with the outline of a lunch box drawn on it. Talk about the different types of food they have been discussing. Say that they are going to make their own lunch box using pictures of food that they find from different sources: magazines, the Internet and their own pictures. Tell them that they must remember the discussions that have already taken place in class and make sure that there is a balance of healthy foods in their lunch box.

When their lunch boxes have been completed, show the children how to make labels for the food in their lunch box using a simple word processing or writing program, such as 'Textease', 'Clicker 4' or 'Talking Write Away'. Show the children how to make the labels using different font sizes, changing the colour and the size of the font. Print out the labels to add to the lunch box.

Name _____

Food and drink

ACTIVITY SHEET 1

To keep fit and healthy we must eat a selection of different foods. Choose from the foods below to make a balanced meal.

Main meal

Dessert

Drink

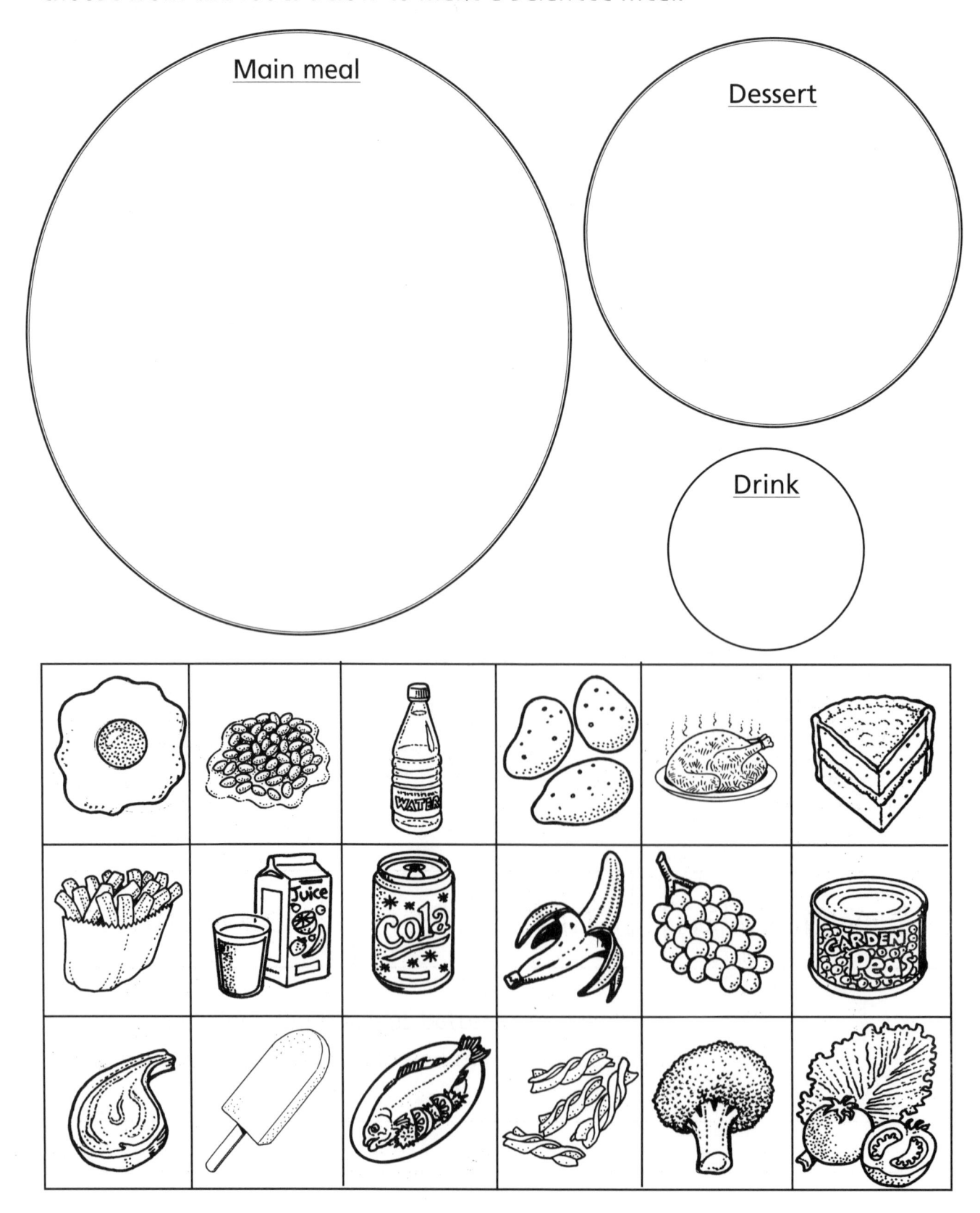

72   CURRICULUM FOCUS • OURSELVES   PHOTOCOPIABLE

Name _____

Food and drink

To keep fit and healthy we must eat a selection of different foods. Here is a choice of foods and drinks.

orange juice   fizzy drink   milk shake   milk
crisps   baked potato   chips   eggs
fish   carrots   pizza   soup
chicken   peas   yoghurt   hamburger
biscuits   apple   banana   cheese
cream cake   tomatoes   lettuce   bread
rice   lamb chops   pasta   chicken   broccoli

Choose from the foods to create a healthy meal. Write or draw it on the menu below.

MENU

PHOTOCOPIABLE

Name _____

Food and drink

ACTIVITY SHEET 3

If we are to keep fit and healthy we must eat a selection of different foods. Here is a choice of foods and drinks.

orange juice	fizzy drink	milk shake	milk
crisps	baked potato	chips	eggs
fish	carrots	pizza	soup
chicken	peas	yoghurt	hamburger
biscuits	apple	banana	cheese
cream cake	tomatoes	lettuce	bread
rice	lamb chops	pasta	chicken	broccoli

Choose your favourite meal. Write it on the menu below.

<u>My favourite meal</u>

Choose a healthy meal. Write it on this menu.

<u>A healthy meal</u>

74 CURRICULUM FOCUS • OURSELVES

PHOTOCOPIABLE

Exercise

TEACHERS' NOTES

Exercise and physical fitness

Unlike a machine, the human body wears out faster when it is idle than when it is used. People in the western world are becoming increasingly sedentary in their work and recreation, and our bodies are adjusting to the lesser demands we make on them. If we laze around for a week, our muscles, heart, lungs and blood circulation adapt to that lethargic situation. Their efficiency decreases drastically because they do not need to be particularly efficient to supply our lower energy requirements. Even the bone marrow produces fewer red blood cells because fewer are being destroyed by activity. When we do start moving around, our body cannot easily adjust to the new situation and so we feel listless and 'washed out'.

There are, therefore, good physiological as well as psychological reasons for taking regular exercise. In the case of children and young people, exercise is essential if they are to achieve full and proper growth. In everyone, young and old, the increased blood flow helps all areas of the body, including the heart, lungs, nervous system, brain and other organs, to become more efficient. At the same time, we recover from injuries and illness quicker if we are physically fit.

Regular exercise reduces the dangerous build up of fatty substances in the blood vessels, and fit people decline more slowly with age. Once physical fitness has been lost, it is difficult to regain. In addition, exercise may provide an essential relaxation from sedentary and stressful occupations, and certain forms of exercise provide social benefits. Finally, and perhaps most importantly, there is a feeling of well-being that comes from being fit.

Exercise and diet

There is a close relationship between exercise and diet. The more physical exercise that is carried out, the more energy-giving foods are required. If the body receives insufficient food energy, then it quickly becomes fatigued. If the body receives more food energy than is required over a long period of time, then the excess food is stored as fat, and obesity may eventually result. If we are trying to build up strength and fitness, and to increase suppleness, then we need to increase the intake of body building protein foods. During increased activity we also need to increase water intake, to compensate for that lost by sweating.

Rest and sleep

Just as important as regular exercise are regular rest and sleep. However, although a great deal is now known about the physiology of rest and sleep, the necessity for them has not yet been fully explained scientifically. What we do know for certain is that during periods of rest the cells of the body are replenished with fuel and building materials, while carbon dioxide and other waste products are removed from them. During sleep, the pulse rate slows, blood pressure falls, the body temperature drops by three to four degrees Celsius, the muscles relax and an essential sequence of sleeping and dreaming takes place. Although the brain becomes much less sensitive to external stimuli during sleep, its activities do not cease.

The traditional views about how much sleep is needed are given less and less credibility today. Research shows that there are very widely differing requirements for sleep in each individual, and social pressures and habits often determine when and for how long people sleep, rather than their bodily needs. In the case of children, only common sense observation will tell whether a child is starting the day refreshed or fatigued. Catnapping – if you can manage it – reduces your night's sleep requirement considerably, as anyone who allows a young child to have a nap during the day will know! By cat-napping during the day you can easily reduce your night sleeping time by half. In order to catnap, though, you must be able to relax very quickly and very efficiently.

Technical terms

Exercise, heat, sweat, sweating, breathing, out of breath, heart, beat, beating, rest, sleep, muscles, active, thirsty.

Exercise

Exercise

	Type of exercise	Length of time
Sunday		
Monday		
Tuesday		
Wednesday		
Thursday		
Friday		
Saturday		

Exercise and sleep

LESSON PLAN

> **Science objectives (Unit 2A)**
> • That we need exercise to stay healthy.

Resources
- The hall or somewhere else where there is plenty or room to move about (Much of this work can be carried out during a PE lesson.)
- Generic sheets 1 and 2 (pages 76 and 77)
- Activity sheets 1 to 3 (pages 80 to 82)

Starting points: *whole class*

Begin by asking the children what they understand by the word 'exercise'. One working definition might be 'an activity that uses our muscles a lot'. Another might be 'an activity that keeps us healthy'. Emphasise that the muscles we use regularly become strong and efficient; those we do not use soon become weak and useless. In other words, help the children to distinguish between being active and being inactive.

Ask the children to stand up and start running on the spot until you say 'stop'. For those children who cannot run, devise another suitable exercise for them to do. When they have stopped, ask:

- How does your skin feel?
- What has happened to your breathing?
- Can you feel your heart?
- Do you feel thirsty?

Ask them to think about the muscles they have been using.

Carry out a class survey of the children's favourite methods of exercising. Record their answers on a tally chart and convert this to a bar chart or histogram or some other visual record.

Go on to tell them that, as well as exercise being good for them, sleep is also good for them. Say it is important that their bodies have long periods of sleep to help them grow and stay healthy. Ask them what time they go to bed. Do they go to sleep straight away or do they read first?

Show the children the pictures of people carrying out various physical activities on Generic sheet 1. Ask them to name each activity and talk about it. Which can you do in the school playground? In the school hall? In the park? In a special building?

Tell them that they are going to do an activity that asks them to identify what is exercise and what is not, and then record information about the exercise they do themselves.

Group activities

Activity sheet 1
This sheet asks the children to identify physical activities, being carried out in a picture, and those activities that are not exercise. They also say what time they go to bed and get up the next day.

Activity sheet 2
This sheet requires the children to identify physical activities and activities that are not exercise from a series of pictures and complete a chart to show their findings. They then have to complete a chart on their own exercise and sleep habits.

Activity sheet 3
This sheet is for the more able children. They have to complete a chart listing activities that are exercise and activities that are not exercise, with no visual clues as the other two sheets have. They then have to complete a diary of their own exercise habits and finally provide information on their sleep habits.

Plenary session

Discuss the effect that exercise has on the body – it makes you hot/sweat, breathe faster, your heart beats faster and your muscles begin to tire. Stress the beneficial effects of exercise in keeping us healthy and fit. Emphasise also that, after exercise, we need to rest and sleep and that children need to rest and sleep more than adults because their bodies are growing.

Go through their responses to the activity sheets, advising those children who don't get enough sleep or exercise that it would be better for them if they did. (Be aware that this might be seen as a criticism of the family, so handle any advice with care.)

Ideas for support

More able children may be able to write about the most enjoyable after-effects of exercise. Less able children may need to draw labelled pictures of themselves after exercise.

Display pictures of the various kinds of exercise and also the class histogram or other visual record of favourite forms of exercise.

Ideas for extension

Calculate the length of time spent doing exercise each week. Use Generic sheet 2 to record this information.

Discuss why we sweat after exercising vigorously, and which parts of the body are particularly affected. Talk about why we should cover ourselves after sweating – particularly on a cold day – and why we need to wash ourselves thoroughly after sweating.

Investigate the effects of exercise on the pulse rate.

Linked ICT activities

Talk to the children about the different games they play in the playground, in PE lessons and on sports day. Start by asking them to think about the different types of sports events they have on school sports day. Give each child a card to hold and to hold it up and give it to you when you call out the name of their favourite sport. Collect the cards as the children hold them up and total the number of children for each activity. (This avoids the children putting their hand up several times and changing the information you are trying to collect.) Tell the children that you are going to put this information into the computer. Explain why you are going to do this – that the computer will help you to see all this information very quickly, and that it can be stored in the computer until you want to look at it again. Use a simple information handling package, such as 'Counter for Windows', to show them how you can put the names of the sports into a list and then add the number of children whose favourite sport it is, at the side of the name. They will then see the information displayed as a list and a graph and can see which is the most favourite and the least favourite sport.

Show the children the chart and start to discuss the results it shows. Why do they think that the most favourite sport in your class is (running)? Why do they think the least favourite is (the sack race)?

Name _____

Exercise and sleep

1 ACTIVITY SHEET

Look at this picture. Colour in red all the people who are exercising and in blue all the people who aren't.

In the boxes below draw a picture of yourself doing two different sorts of exercise. Write how long you do it for.

| I do this for _____ minutes. | I do this for _____ minutes. |

What time do you go to bed? _____

What time do you get up? _____

80 CURRICULUM FOCUS • OURSELVES

PHOTOCOPIABLE

Name _____

Exercise and sleep

2 ACTIVITY SHEET

Look at these pictures. Complete the chart below to show whether each is an exercise or not.

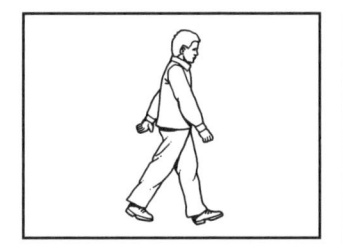

Exercise	Not exercise

Which exercise do you do?
_____

How long for each week?
_____

What time do you go to bed?
_____

What time do you get up?
_____

How many hours do you sleep each night?
_____

PHOTOCOPIABLE

CURRICULUM FOCUS • OURSELVES 81

Name _____

Exercise and sleep

3 ACTIVITY SHEET

Complete the chart below. Two have been done for you.

Exercise	Not exercise
playing football	reading a book

Complete the diary below to show when you exercise, what you do and for how long.

	Type of exercise	How long for
Monday		
Tuesday		
Wednesday		
Thursday		
Friday		
Saturday		
Sunday		

What time do you go to bed? _____

What time do you get up? _____

How many hours do you sleep each night? _____

CURRICULUM FOCUS • OURSELVES

PHOTOCOPIABLE

Medicines and drugs

CHAPTER 9

TEACHERS' NOTES

Drugs and medicines

A drug is any substance, natural or synthetic, which has an effect on the functioning of the body. By this definition, substances such as alcohol, the nicotine from tobacco, and the solvents of glues and other substances are drugs. A medicine has a much more restricted definition. It is any substance taken into the body which has a curative or beneficial effect, such as in relieving pain or treating illness. Thus all medicines are drugs, but not all drugs are medicines.

There are many drugs which some people take every day. Caffeine in coffee and cola drinks, and to a lesser extent in tea, and the alcohol in alcoholic drinks, are stimulant drugs. In small doses they may not be harmful, but large doses over a long period can be dangerous.

Alcohol

People first learned to make alcoholic drinks thousands of years ago. The type of alcohol in wine, beer and spirits is ethanol. It is a drug that is absorbed through the stomach into the bloodstream, which explains its rapid effects. Alcohol can affect the nervous system, with small quantities working as a stimulant, while larger amounts are a sedative. Alcohol changes a person's view of the world – distances are judged wrongly, reactions are slowed, walking and standing become difficult, and eventually the person falls asleep. As with many drugs, people can become dependent on alcohol and are then known as alcoholics. An alcoholic may suffer from vitamin and other deficiency diseases, since the alcohol can be used as food in the body but does not provide essential vitamins and minerals. The liver is seriously damaged by large amounts of alcohol, a condition known as cirrhosis of the liver. Heart disease and stomach ulcers are just two more of the health problems that can arise from the misuse of alcohol. Social problems, such as violence, crime and damage to the family can also result from alcohol abuse.

Nicotine

The nicotine in tobacco smoke, either breathed in deliberately or passively, is also an addictive drug. It paralyses the cilia lining the breathing passages and can cause difficulty in breathing, a smoker's cough or even bronchitis. Sometimes during violent coughing induced by smoking, the air sacs of the lungs burst. This means that there is less surface area in the lungs for oxygen and carbon dioxide to be exchanged. This illness is called emphysema.

The problems do not end there. The carbon monoxide gas in tobacco smoke gets into the blood and combines with the red pigment haemoglobin, making it more difficult for the red blood cells to pick up oxygen. At the same time, the tar in tobacco smoke sticks in the air sacs of the lungs, irritating them, and eventually causing lung cancer in some people. There is definite evidence that, on average, people who smoke die 10 years younger than non-smokers.

Solvents

The solvents in glue, lighter fuel, paint thinners and household dry cleaning agents can also enter the blood via the lungs if they are sniffed. These chemicals are poisonous and can cause hallucinations, mental confusion, brain damage or even death. There have also been a number of instances where 'solvent sniffers' have suffocated from inhaling their own vomit or by falling unconscious while their heads have been covered by a plastic bag.

Finally, it should be remembered that all drugs are chemicals that can change the way the body works. All drugs and medicines involve a risk, and dosage instructions must be followed carefully. The body can become tolerant to some drugs, so that larger doses are needed to produce the same effect. As can be seen in the case of nicotine and alcohol, some people quickly become addicted to drugs.

Prescription and non-prescription medicines

There are two classes of medicines available legally. Non-prescription (or 'over the counter') medicines include cough and cold remedies, painkillers, antiseptics, and vitamin and nutritional supplements. Although these are often widely available, it is important for children to realise that these too can be dangerous if taken inappropriately, or if the stated dosage is exceeded. Virtually all oral medicines are designed to be taken in particular dosages at a given time and over a given period, while creams and ointments for external use may be dangerous if taken internally.

There is, in addition, a wide range of medicines that may be prescribed to treat specific medical conditions. Again, it is important to remember that these are prescribed for a particular person, for a particular condition, and the dosage should not be exceeded at any given time nor should the medicine be taken more frequently or for longer than the stipulated period. There are, for example, well documented cases where patients have become addicted after prolonged use of certain anti-depressants and tranquillisers.

Taking medicines

There are different ways of introducing medicines into the body. The three main ways that are used are by mouth, by injection and through the skin.

The time taken for a medicine to work depends on the amount of medicine taken and the way it is put into the body. A larger amount will produce a quicker and longer lasting effect than a small one. A medicine that is injected will show its effect quickly as it is put straight into the blood. One that is swallowed may not produce its effect for half an hour or more as it has to pass through the wall of the gut to reach the blood.

A medicine put on the skin may also produce an immediate, if localised effect. Zinc ointment for sore, moist skin, or soft lanolin for itching and sunburn may produce their effects immediately. By contrast the 'nicotine patches', designed to help reduce the urge to smoke tobacco, 'leak' the nicotine into the body slowly so that their effect is more prolonged.

Most young children have had experience of injections in the form of vaccinations. A vaccine contains dead or harmless versions of the disease-producing organism. These do not produce the illness (though they may produce some of its minor symptoms), but they stimulate the body's immune system to produce the same defensive cells and antibodies that the active organism does. These cells and antibodies stay in the bloodstream, ready to defend the body if a real infection takes place. Today most children are offered a series of vaccinations, usually by injection, which prevent them developing such potentially dangerous infectious diseases as diphtheria, whooping cough, polio, tuberculosis, measles and rubella (German measles). Those planning to travel abroad may additionally be given vaccinations against such diseases as yellow fever, cholera, typhoid and meningitis.

Many other medicines are given in tablet or capsule form. They include most of the different antibiotic drugs that are available to fight bacterial infections. Analgesic drugs (pain relievers) such as aspirin, paracetamol and codeine are also normally given in tablet form.

Another way to give a drug by mouth is in the form of an inhaler. An asthma attack, for example, can be relieved by breathing in a drug from an inhaler that relaxes the muscles in the airway walls, allowing them to open up.

Technical terms

Pills, medicine, tablets, drugs, ill, doctor, nurse, ointment, needle, syringe, inhaler, breathe, vaccination, swallow, swallowing, germs, danger, poison, caution.

Taking medicines

LESSON PLAN 1

Science objectives (Unit 2A)
- That sometimes we take medicines when we get ill; they help us to get better.
- That medicines are useful but are drugs not foods, and can be dangerous.
- That some people need medicines to keep them alive and healthy.

Resources
- Clean, empty medicine containers, including empty pill and medicine bottles, vitamin and eye drop bottles, an asthma inhaler, a blister pack for tablets; ointment tubes, plastic syringes (without needles), droppers, medicine spoons, plastic drinking glasses
- Activity sheets 1–3 (pages 87–89)

Starting points: *whole class*

Begin by discussing what it is like to be ill. How do we know we are ill? What does it feel like? What does a doctor do to find out what is wrong with us? What does the doctor do to make us feel better?

Talk about medicines. What is a medicine and why do we take medicines? Explain that some people, such as diabetics and asthmatics, have to take medicines regularly to keep them alive. Where do we obtain medicines? Ask the children to describe medicines they have been given by a parent, carer, doctor or nurse. Why were they given the medicines? How did these medicines enter their bodies (injecting, swallowing, breathing in, through the skin)? Record their experiences with medicines on the board.

Pass the containers around for the children to examine. Allow them to investigate the syringes, medicine spoons and droppers by filling them with water and transferring it to and from a plastic drinking glass. How much water does each type of container hold? Why does an eye dropper hold less water than a syringe? Talk about the materials used to make the containers. Why are syringes and droppers made of transparent plastic? Why are ointment tubes flexible?

Throughout the activity stress the important safety messages, including:

- Never touch a syringe you find. It might hurt you or have germs in it.
- Never take medicines unless they are given to you by a trusted adult.
- Things that look like sweets may not be sweets and could make you ill.

Group activities

Activity sheet 1
This sheet asks the children to correctly link six types of medicine with the ways in which they are applied or are taken.

Activity sheet 2
This sheet asks the children to correctly link six types of medicine with the ways in which they are applied or are taken. They are then asked to name two people from whom they may accept medicines.

Activity sheet 3
This sheet is for the more able children. They are required to correctly link six types of medicine with the ways in which they are applied or taken. They have to name two people from whom they may accept medicines and then describe two occasions when medicines may be harmful.

Plenary session

Ask the children to tell you why you might need medicines, when it is safe to take them and who should give you the medicines. Stress that medicines can be dangerous unless given under adult supervision. Describe how some people need to take, or be given medicines, to keep them alive. What are some of the words that are found on medicine containers?

Ideas for support

Make an exhibition of the medicine containers.

Make a large collage picture of a chemist's shop to illustrate the source of many drugs and medicines and to emphasise the wide range of containers in whch drugs and medicines are available.

Ideas for extension

Discuss with the children where they would go for help if they felt unwell or had a minor injury.

Use the medical room or provide the home corner with a make shift bed. Ask pairs of children to role play being patients and doctors.

Linked ICT activities

Ask the children if they have ever visited the doctor. (Be sensitive to the fact that some of them may not have happy memories of visits to the doctor; for example, if a member of the family has been seriously ill.) Talk about what happens when we go to the doctor. The person at reception will ask for your name and put all of your information into the computer. Talk about why the receptionist takes your name, and what happens when they put your name into the computer?

Set up a role play area in the classroom. Put a computer or an old laptop in this area. Give the children the opportunity to act out the role of the receptionist in the doctor's surgery and use the computer to type in the names of the person coming to the doctor's. This could be done using a simple word processing program, such as 'Textease' or 'Talking Write Away'.

Show the children the program 'At the Doctor's' (Granada Learning, Semerc) and set this up in the role play area. This program is designed to support the activity of role play in a doctor's surgery and will allow the children to take on the role of the doctor's receptionist.

Name _____

Taking medicines

ACTIVITY SHEET 1

Here are some ways we can take medicines.
Draw a line to join the medicine to how it is taken.

| on the skin | swallowed | breathed in |

| swallowed | in the skin | swallowed |

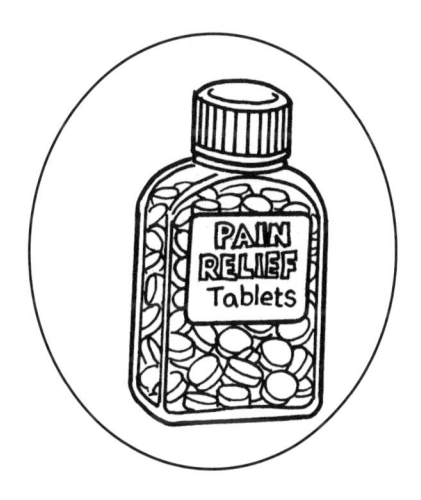

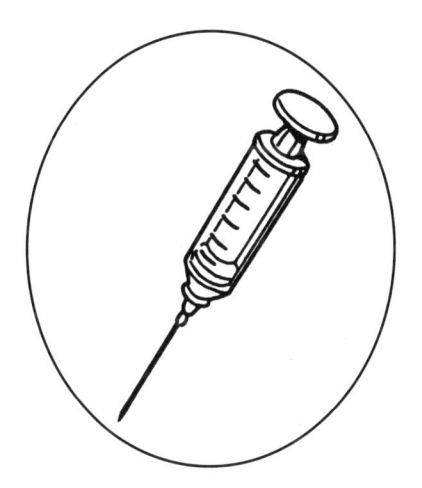

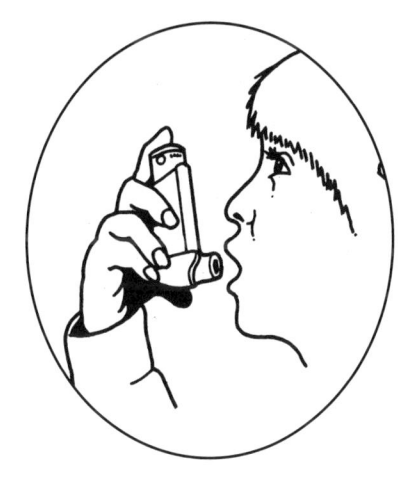

PHOTOCOPIABLE

CURRICULUM FOCUS • OURSELVES 87

Name _____

Taking medicines

ACTIVITY SHEET 2

Here are some ways we can take medicines.
Draw a line to join the medicine to how it is taken.

| on the skin | swallowed | breathed in |

| swallowed | in the skin | swallowed |

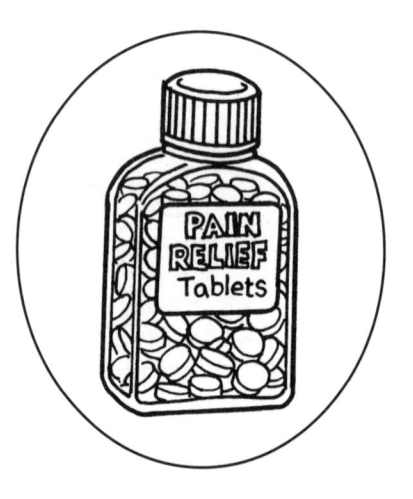

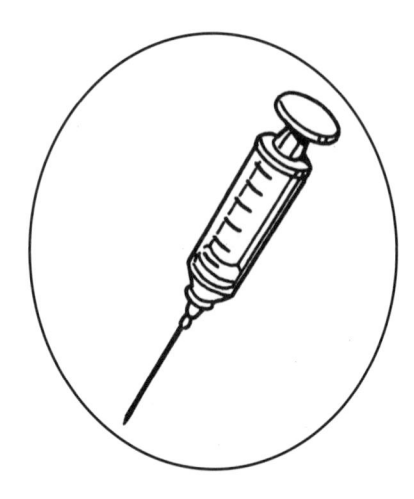

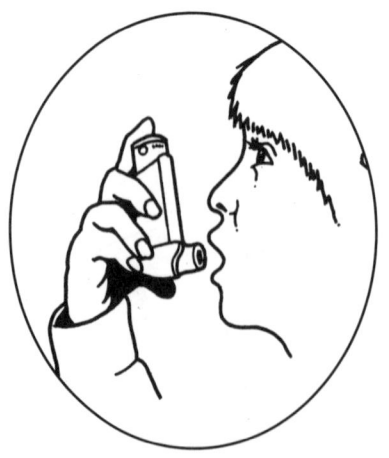

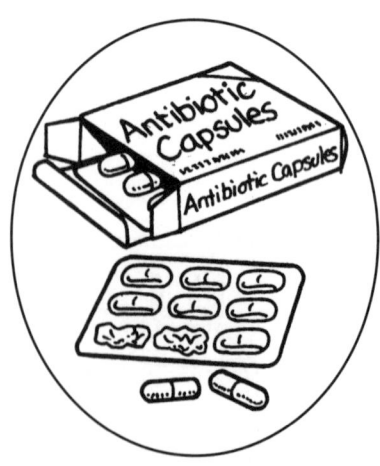

All these medicines can make us better if we are ill.
Name two people who are allowed to give us medicines.

a) _____

b) _____

Name _____

Taking medicines

ACTIVITY SHEET 3

Here are some ways we can take medicines. Under each picture, write how the medicine is taken.

WORD BANK
on the skin   swallowed   breathed in   in the skin

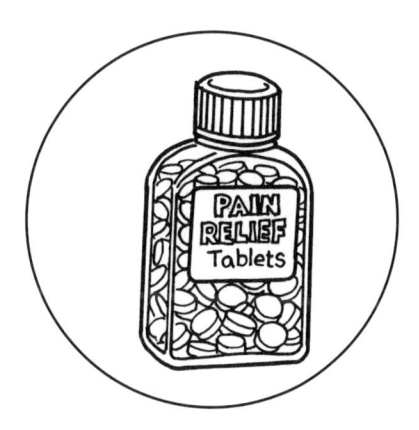

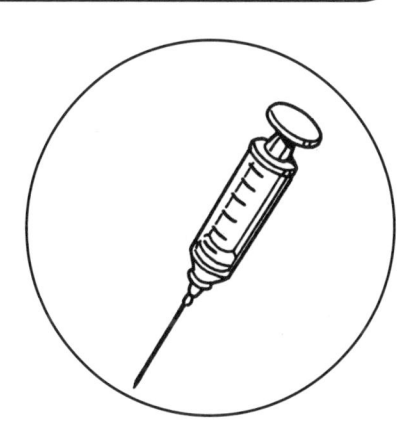

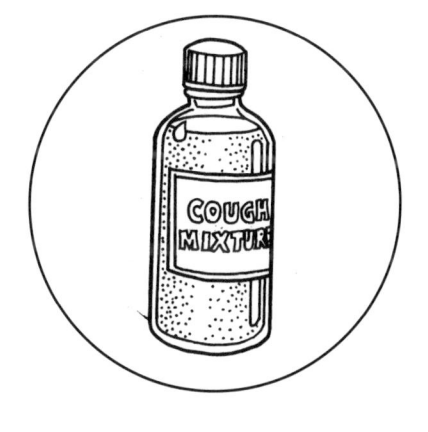

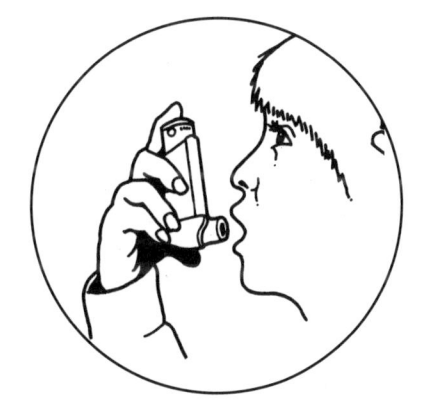

_____   _____   _____

_____   _____   _____

Name two people who are allowed to give us medicines.

a) _____

b) _____

When could medicines be harmful to us?

a) _____

b) _____

PHOTOCOPIABLE   CURRICULUM FOCUS • OURSELVES   89

LESSON PLAN 2

Using medicines safely

Science objectives (Unit 2A)
- To know that we take medicines when we are ill; they help us to get better.
- To know that medicines can be dangerous if we take them without consulting parents or doctors.
- To recognise the hazards and risks in medicines and how to avoid these.

Resources
- A collection of empty sweet packets, tubes, boxes and wrappers
- Clean, empty medicine containers, including empty pill and medicine bottles, vitamin and eye drop bottles, an asthma inhaler, a blister pack for tablets; ointment tubes, plastic syringes (without needles)
- (Optional) some bright coloured tablets (iron tablets or multivitamin tablets) and some small coloured sweets, such as Smarties

Starting points: *whole class*

One common reason for children having to visit hospital is because they have swallowed some tablets or some other medicine they have discovered in their home.

One way to introduce this important area of work is to arrange two identical tables at the front of the classroom. Cover one table with red cloth or paper, the other with green cloth or paper. These are the 'Unsafe' and 'Safe' tables.

Hold up the sweet containers or wrappers or the medicine containers, one at a time. The children have to decide on which table – 'Safe' or 'Unsafe' – the container should go. They should be told that if they are unsure about a container, then it should go on the 'Unsafe' table. Show them the tablets that look like sweets and explain that they are not sweets, but could be very harmful if they were eaten.

(This might be the time to talk about the abuse of drugs, such as alcohol and cigarettes. Individual teachers will know how best to address this. Consult your school's guidelines.)

Tell the children that they are going to do an activity that will show if they understand about how safe or dangerous medicines and drugs can be.

Group activities

Activity sheet 1
This sheet asks the children to examine six pictures of children being exposed to medicines, and to say which children are acting safely and which are acting dangerously.

Activity sheet 2
This sheet requires the children to examine six pictures of children being exposed to medicines, and to indicate which children are acting safely and which are acting dangerously. They are then asked to describe what they should do if they found some sweets on their way to school.

Activity sheet 3
This sheet is for more able children. They are required to examine six pictures of children being exposed to medicines, and to then explain why what some of the children are doing is safe, while others are acting dangerously. The children are also asked to describe what they should do if they found some sweets on their way to school.

Plenary session

Discuss with the class what they have learned. Draw up a set of rules concerning the safe use of medicines. The rules could include the following.

- Only take medicines if a responsible adult, such as a parent, carer, doctor or nurse gives them to you.
- Never touch medicines, tablets or their containers unless a trusted and responsible adult is present.
- Never take medicines intended for someone else.

- Never touch a syringe, but tell a responsible adult where you saw it.
- Never eat things you find, even if they look like sweets.
- Do not try to open childproof bottle caps – they are there to protect you.
- Never go to the medicine cabinet or first aid box without the help of a responsible adult.

Ideas for support

Display the 'Safe' and 'Unsafe' tables for your own class and other classes to see.

Encourage the children to make a poster that illustrates one of the rules about the safe use of medicines.

Ideas for extension

Invite the school nurse, the district nurse, or a parent who is a nurse or doctor to come to the classroom and to display and explain the safe use of medical or first aid items.

Tell the children that medicines are not the only substances where great care is needed. Ask the children to describe some of the ways in which household and garden substances can be dangerous (poisonous; damage the skin; may catch fire). Introduce them to the three main warning symbols (Harmful or Irritant, Toxic, or Highly Flammable) that often appear on household and garden chemical containers.

Linked ICT activities

Talk to the children about using medicines safely and what we mean by 'safe' medicines. Tell them that they are going to create a poster to display around school to help other children in school to understand what is meant by safe medicines. Talk about some of the key things that should go on the poster. Write down some of the key words the children suggest, using the whiteboard or flip chart. Put some of these words into sentences. Discuss with the children the sentences and headings that they could add to the poster to show show their key messages. They could create their poster using pictures from magazines, adding their labels and sentences, which could be created using a word processing program such as 'Textease', 'Talking Write Away' or 'Clicker 4'.

Name _____

Using medicines safely

Look at the pictures.

Which of the children are using medicines safely? (Put a tick.)

Which of the children are using medicines dangerously? (Put a cross.)

ACTIVITY SHEET 1

92 CURRICULUM FOCUS • OURSELVES

PHOTOCOPIABLE

Name _____

Using medicines safely

2 ACTIVITY SHEET

Look at the pictures.
Which of the children are using medicines safely? (Put a tick.)
Which of the children are using medicines dangerously? (Put a cross.)

What should you do if you find some sweets on your way to school?

_____

_____

PHOTOCOPIABLE

CURRICULUM FOCUS • OURSELVES   93

Name _____

Using medicines safely

3
ACTIVITY SHEET

Which of the children are using medicines safely or dangerously?
Say why what they are doing is safe or dangerous.

_____	_____
_____	_____
_____	_____

What should you do if you find some sweets on your way to school?

_____

_____

_____

94   CURRICULUM FOCUS • OURSELVES

PHOTOCOPIABLE